The Shores of a Dream

Yasuo Kuniyoshi's Early Work in America

This photograph of Yasuo Kuniyoshi (left), Katherine Schmidt (second from left), and two friends
(possibly Dorothy Varian and Robert Laurent) was taken at Ogunquit, Maine, in 1922 or 1923.
Carl Zigrosser Papers, Special Collections, Van Pelt Library, University of Pennsylvania

The Shores
of a Dream

Yasuo Kuniyoshi's
Early Work in America

Essays by

JANE MYERS & TOM WOLF

AMON CARTER MUSEUM
Fort Worth, Texas

©1996, Amon Carter Museum

Published in conjunction with the exhibition, *The Shores of a Dream: The Early Work of Yasuo Kuniyoshi*

Amon Carter Museum, Fort Worth, Texas
September 7 - November 17, 1996

Portland Museum of Art, Portland, Maine
February 1 - March 30, 1997

ISBN 0-88360-086-2

Library of Congress Cataloging-in-Publication Data
Myers, Jane, 1955–
    The shores of a dream : Yasuo Kuniyoshi's early work in America / essays by Jane Myers and Tom Wolf.
        p. cm.
    Includes index.
    ISBN 0-88360-086-2 (softcover)
    1. Kuniyoshi, Yasuo, 1889-1953—Criticism and interpretation.
I. Wolf, Tom. II. Title.
N6537.K83M94   1996
759.13—dc20   96-31120
                                                              CIP

Edited by Nancy Stevens
Designed by Tom Dawson Graphic Design, Dallas, Texas
Halftones and composite film by CBS of Arlington, Arlington, Texas
Separations by Harper House, Dallas, Texas
Printed by Authentic Press, Arlington, Texas

COVER:
Yasuo Kuniyoshi, *The Swimmer*, c. 1924, oil on canvas, Columbus Museum of Art, Columbus, Ohio, gift of Ferdinand Howald

Contents

INTRODUCTION

vi

ACKNOWLEDGMENTS

viii

COLOR PLATES

1

KUNIYOSHI IN THE EARLY 1920s

Tom Wolf

21

PLATES

43

INDEPENDENT CREATIONS:
KUNIYOSHI'S INK DRAWINGS OF 1921-25

Jane Myers

55

INDEX

70

Introduction

When he immigrated to the United States, Yasuo Kuniyoshi (1889-1953) envisioned America as the answer to his youthful dreams. He attributed his initial desire to travel to foreign lands, where they spoke languages he did not comprehend, to childhood memories of the Westerners he encountered in the seventeenth-century garden near his home in Okayama, Japan. Like other Japanese men of his generation, he also perceived America as a land of opportunity. High unemployment following the Russo-Japanese War (1904-05) enticed many to America with romantic notions of material success. Over 8,400 Japanese immigrated to the United States in 1906, the year Kuniyoshi and many from his home prefecture, Okayama, disembarked on this continent.[1] Kuniyoshi had to hold his dreams of affluence in abeyance, however, spending several years at manual labor as a railroad and field worker in the American West and Northwest.

Like many *Issei* (first-generation Japanese Americans), Kuniyoshi intended to stay in the United States merely long enough to achieve prosperity. Instead, he returned to Japan only once, in 1931. By then a highly esteemed and successful New York artist, he experienced a surprising degree of discomfort in his native country. Returning to the United States following this visit with his family, he embraced his adopted homeland with relief: "Once again I touched the shores of my childhood dreams, this time greeted by friends and delighted to be back in a land that no longer seemed strange."[2]

Kuniyoshi's fusion of Asian and American principles can be seen in the artist's first mature artistic efforts. This exhibition focuses on those early works—a small selection of his oil paintings and ink drawings from the early 1920s. Their idiosyncratic imagery is often tantalizingly obscure. Perhaps because of the language barrier he

Yasuo Kuniyoshi, *Forbidden Fruit*, 1950, oil on canvas, 44¼ x 62⅜ in. (112.4 x 158.4 cm),
Courtesy of the Syracuse University Art Collection

Yasuo Kuniyoshi, *Revelation*, 1949, oil on canvas, 69½ x 49½ in. (176.5 x 125.7 cm), Wichita Art Museum, Wichita, Kansas, The Roland P. Murdock Collection

plished of these works, the whimsical *Boy Stealing Fruit* (1923, pl. 5), for example, suggests an archetypical connotation which Kuniyoshi recast in more sobering tones in *Forbidden Fruit* during the 1950s—another particularly strong period for the artist.

Determined to become an American success, but often inspired by his Japanese heritage, Kuniyoshi had to weather the historical anti-Asian prejudices in America, perhaps most keenly felt during World War II. Yet the mature Kuniyoshi enjoyed popularity as an artist, teacher, and advocate for artists' rights until his death in 1953, at age 63. Interest in him then waned until 1973, when his work commanded high prices at the estate auction of Edith Gregor Halpert, his dealer for much of his career. To the astonishment of many, *Little Joe with Cow*, a 1923 oil (private collection, Japan), brought $220,000, setting a record for a twentieth-century American work of art.[5]

Most buyers of Kuniyoshi's work at the Halpert sale were Japanese collectors discovering his paintings for the first time, and among them the artist fast became a favorite. Since 1973, Japanese institutions and private collectors have remained interested in his work, and a large body of it is now in Japan, particularly at the Yasuo Kuniyoshi Museum in Okayama, his hometown.[6] That the Japanese would eventually recognize and appreciate his unique sensibility is something that American art critic Henry McBride anticipated in 1925, when he wrote that Kuniyoshi's native countrymen "haven't seen many yet, naturally, since most of these first rate works of art are still with us, but the time will come, assuredly, when the Japanese will share with us an admiration for this joint product of the two nations."[7]

initially experienced, Kuniyoshi wrote little during the 1920s, leaving room for creative speculation. His early works appear to embody a uniquely bicultural quality which he would address more explicitly in such powerful works as *Revelation* (1949), made following the tumult and political pressures of World War II. Kuniyoshi later characterized his early work as being drawn from the world of ideas and memories, whereas after he went to Paris in 1925, his style became more Western and realistic.[3] Clearly, the early imagery, with its poetic world of fantasy, had a particular resonance for him, because towards the end of his career, he commented that he sought to return to the realm of ideas from which he had drawn his early paintings.[4] One of the most accom-

1   Kuniyoshi recalled that many people from Okayama Prefecture came to the United States (Lloyd Goodrich Archives from Whitney Museum of American Art, Archives of American Art, reel N-670, frames 55-56). See also Lauren Kessler, *Stubborn Twig: Three Generations in the Life of a Japanese American Family* (New York: Random House, 1993), pp. 5, 12.

2   Yasuo Kuniyoshi, "East to West," *Magazine of Art* 33 (February 1940): 81.

3   Goodrich Archives, AAA, reel N-670, frames 58 and 62.

4   Ibid, frame 62.

5   In the same sale, Stuart Davis' masterpiece *Hot Still-Scape for Six Colors—Seventh Ave. Style* (1940, Museum of Fine Arts, Boston) sold for $175,000. Judith Tannenbaum, "The Dominance of Diversity," *Arts Magazine* 47 (May-June 1973): 70-71.

6   The Kuniyoshi Museum has issued a catalogue raisonné of the artist's paintings. Titles are given in English and Japanese, but text is in Japanese only. See *Yasuo Kuniyoshi* (Okayama: Fukutake Publishing Company, Ltd., 1991).

7   Henry McBride, unidentified clipping, January 3, 1925, Yasuo Kuniyoshi Papers, Archives of American Art, reel D-176, frame 167.

Acknowledgments

. . . .

The Amon Carter Museum is grateful to the lending institutions and their staffs for making this exhibition possible. The works reproduced in the plate section represent substantial efforts by curators, registrars, and photographers of the Archer M. Huntington Art Gallery, The University of Texas at Austin; The Art Institute of Chicago; Bridgestone Museum of Art, Ishibashi Foundation; The Brooklyn Museum; The Cleveland Museum of Art; Columbus Museum of Art; The Corcoran Gallery of Art; The Currier Gallery of Art; Dallas Museum of Art; Denver Art Museum; Elvehjem Museum of Art, University of Wisconsin-Madison; Fine Arts Museums of San Francisco; Indianapolis Museum of Art; The Metropolitan Museum of Art, New York; The Museum of Modern Art, New York; The Ogunquit Museum of American Art; Portland Museum of Art; The Phillips Collection; The Regis Collection; Robert Hull Fleming Museum, University of Vermont; The Saint Louis Art Museum; Smith College Museum of Art; Yasuo Kuniyoshi Museum, Okayama, Japan; The University of Iowa Museum of Art; Wadsworth Atheneum; and the Whitney Museum of American Art. We extend our particular thanks to Ritsuko T. Ozawa, curator of the Yasuo Kuniyoshi Museum, who has been an important advocate for the exhibition.

Tom Wolf, the leading American Kuniyoshi scholar and catalogue essayist, has provided generous and wise counsel, and the two essays in this catalogue have greatly benefitted from the mutual nature of the project. We extend our special thanks to Sara Mazo Kuniyoshi, whose gracious support and assistance have been of great value, and to Cheryl Wolf.

The Shores of a Dream: Yasuo Kuniyoshi's Early Work in America is organized by the Amon Carter Museum in association with Sun & Star 1996. The exhibition and accompanying publication are funded in part by Mitsubishi Heavy Industries, Ltd., through their support of Sun & Star 1996, the National Endowment for the Arts, and the Katrine Menzing Deakins Charitable Trust, NationsBank, trustee. The Founding Sponsors for Sun & Star 1996 are EDS and Hitachi, Ltd.

Other individuals who have generously lent their time and expertise include Judy Throm, Archives of American Art; Mark Pascale, The Art Institute of Chicago; Kathie and Scott Bennewitz; the staff of Botanical Research Institute, Fort Worth, Texas; Sandy Brook; Lynn Marsden-Atlass, Colby College Museum of Art; Janis Conner; Andrew Spahr and Michele Marcantonio, The Currier Gallery of Art; David and Sibley Dittmer; Ann Yonemura, Freer Gallery of Art; Hisako Hanson, Sun & Star 1996; Warren S. Hallamore; Jennifer R. Casler, Kimbell Art Museum; Paul Laurent; John Laurent; Isabel Lewando; Mary Lublin; Liz Lunning and Judy Gibbs, The Menil Collection; Judy Walsh, National Gallery of Art, Washington, D. C.; Shigenobu Kimura, The National Museum of Art, Osaka; Shinji Kohmoto, The National Museum of Modern Art, Kyoto; Joel and Mary Kate Myers; Heather B. Nevin; Michael Culver, The Ogunquit Museum of American Art; Masako Yamamoto, Okayama Institute of Languages; Michael Owen; Jessica F. Nicoll, Portland Museum of Art; Gennifer Weisenfeld, Princeton University; Franklin Riehlman; Joel Rosenkranz; Katsko Suzuki; Siri Engberg, Walker Art Center; and Richard York.

As always, the staff of the Amon Carter Museum has made innumerable contributions to this exhibition and publication with exemplary talent and good spirit. My particular gratitude goes to Rick Stewart, Bob Workman, Nancy Stevens, Jane Posey, Melissa Thompson, Chris Rauhoff, and Cliff Dossel, for their careful stewardship of this project to date.

JANE MYERS
Chief Curator

PLATE 1

Adam and Eve (The Fall of Man), 1922, oil on canvas,
20 x 30 in. (50.8 x 76.2 cm), private collection, New York

2

PLATE 2

Dream, 1922, oil on canvas, 20¼ x 30⅛ in. (51.5 x 76.7 cm),
Bridgestone Museum of Art, Ishibashi Foundation, Tokyo

PLATE 3

Upstream, 1922, oil on canvas, 30¼ x 24⅜ in.
(76.7 x 60.8 cm), Denver Art Museum

4

Plate 4

Maine Family, 1922-23, oil on canvas, 30 x 24 in.
(76.2 x 60.9 cm), The Phillips Collection, Washington, D.C.

PLATE 5

Boy Stealing Fruit, 1923, oil on canvas, 20 x 30 in.
(50.8 x 76.2 cm), Columbus Museum of Art, Columbus,
Ohio, gift of Ferdinand Howald

P<small>LATE</small> **6**

Cows in Pasture, 1923, oil on canvas, 20 x 30 in.
(50.8 x 76.2 cm), Collection of the Corcoran Gallery of Art,
Washington, D.C., gift of George Biddle

PLATE 7

After the Bath, 1923, oil on canvas, 30⅛ x 24⅛ in.
(76.5 x 61.3 cm), Portland Museum of Art, Portland, Maine,
Hamilton Easter Field Art Foundation Collection,
gift of Barn Gallery Associates, Ogunquit, Maine

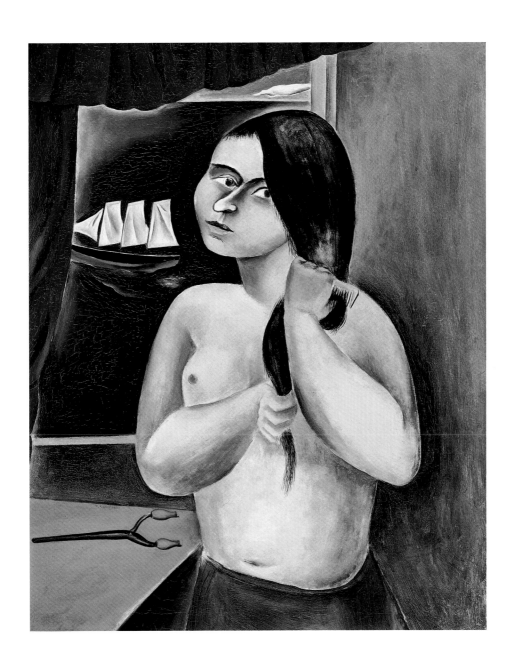

8

PLATE **8**

Fish and Seaweed, 1923, oil on canvas, 30 x 20 in.
(76.2 x 50.8 cm), The Regis Collection, Minneapolis,
Minnesota

PLATE 9

Life Saver, 1924, oil on canvas, 30⅛ in. x 25 in.
(76.5 x 63.5 cm), Yasuo Kuniyoshi Museum,
Okayama, Japan, Benesse Collection

PLATE 10

Bather with Cigarette, 1924, oil on canvas, 42 x 25 in.
(106.7 x 63.5 cm), Dallas Museum of Art, Dallas Art
Association Purchase Fund, Deaccession Funds/City of Dallas
(by exchange), in honor of Dr. Steven A. Nash

PLATE 11

The Swimmer, c. 1924, oil on canvas, 20½ x 30½ in.
(52.1 x 77.5 cm), Columbus Museum of Art, Columbus,
Ohio, gift of Ferdinand Howald

PLATE 12

Self-Portrait as a Photographer, 1924, oil on canvas,
20⅜ x 30¼ in. (51.8 x 76.8 cm), The Metropolitan Museum
of Art, New York, bequest of Scofield Thayer, 1982

PLATE 13

Waitresses from the Sparhawk, 1924/25, oil on canvas,
29 ⅜ x 41½ in. (74.6 x 105.4 cm), Archer M. Huntington
Art Gallery, The University of Texas at Austin,
gift of Mari and James A. Michener, 1991

14

Plate 14

Grapes in White Bowl, 1923, pen and ink, brush and ink, colored ink, and graphite on paper, 22⅛ x 15¼ in. (56.7 x 39.2 cm), Wadsworth Atheneum, Hartford, Connecticut, gift of William E. Hill

PLATE 15

Pear, 1923, pen and ink, brush and ink, graphite,
and watercolor on paper, 22⁵⁄₁₆ x 15⁷⁄₁₆ in.
(56.7 x 39.1 cm), The Cleveland Museum of Art,
gift of Mrs. Malcolm L. McBride

PLATE 16

Dish with Banana, 1923, pen and ink, brush and ink, colored
inks, and graphite on paper, 20¹⁄₁₆ x 15³⁄₁₆ in. (51.2 x 38.6 cm),
The Art Institute of Chicago, gift of The Arts Club of Chicago

PLATE 17

Lady Slipper, 1924, pen and ink, brush and ink, and watercolor on paper, 20 x 13¾ in. (50.8 x 34.9 cm), Whitney Museum of American Art, New York, gift of Gertrude Vanderbilt Whitney

18

PLATE **18**

Leaves in a Vase, 1924, pen and ink, brush and ink, watercolor,
and graphite on paper, 19¾ x 14⅜ in. (50.4 x 36.5 cm),
Fine Arts Museums of San Francisco, Achenbach Foundation
for Graphic Arts, gift of the Graphic Arts Council

PLATE 19

Squash, 1924, pen and ink, brush and ink, colored ink,
and graphite on paper, 15¼ x 22¼ in.
(38.7 x 56.5 cm), Indianapolis Museum of Art,
The Robert and Traude Hensel Collection

20

PLATE 20

Orange, 1925, pen and ink, brush and ink, and colored ink
on paper, 14¼ x 18⅞ in. (36.2 x 47.9 cm), Collection of
Warren S. Hallamore, courtesy of The Currier Gallery of Art,
Manchester, New Hampshire

Kuniyoshi in the
Early 1920s

. . . .

Tom Wolf

When Yasuo Kuniyoshi moved to New York, the nation's artistic capital, to study art in 1910, that city was about to enter a new phase of artistic vitality. The famous Armory Show of 1913 would introduce European avant-garde art to a shocked, unprepared public and rack up tremendous attendance figures. During World War I, leading figures from the School of Paris would take up residence in New York, disseminating their radical aesthetic ideas. Many young American artists who settled there had already visited Europe, and following the example of European modernists who had explored previously ignored aspects of indigenous artistic traditions, they started looking seriously at American folk art. New York offered a young artist stimulation and artistic variety to the point of bewilderment. In the midst of this ferment, Kuniyoshi found his own voice—a voice that would lead to his becoming one of the most esteemed painters in the United States in the 1930s and 1940s, before the onslaught of Abstract Expressionism.

Kuniyoshi's style first crystallized in the early 1920s, when he created paintings and drawings of great charm, beauty, and originality. He drew from many stimuli, including the more conservative tendencies of American modernism that have received little scholarly attention since World War II. His Japanese heritage also affected his art, although the exact meaning of this frequently invoked legacy has seldom been analyzed. The essay that follows will attempt to understand Kuniyoshi's development in these crucial years and to define the rich artistic milieu that stimulated him to create brilliantly expressive works in the early 1920s.

Kuniyoshi's independent personality was evident in his youth. In 1906, just before he turned seventeen, he left his parents and his hometown of Okayama, Japan, and set off alone for America. He had taken classes in weaving, dyeing, and textile design in Japan, though he had no intention of becoming an artist until after he

moved to the United States. In his major autobiographical statement he recalled seeing a realistic Western-style painting when he was a young boy: "It stirred me greatly because it was so real and life-like, a factor I had not been aware of in the works of art that surrounded me in my childhood."[1] While announcing his early attraction to non-Asian art, this statement also establishes that he was well aware of Japanese art before leaving his native country, where he felt he was "surrounded" by it.

A teacher in a Los Angeles high school encouraged him to pursue art, and in 1907 Kuniyoshi enrolled at the Los Angeles School of Art and Design. His ambition grew, and in 1910 he left most of his fellow Japanese immigrants behind on the West Coast and traveled cross-country to New York, where he was exposed to the heady, dynamic world of American art at the moment it encountered European modernism. Immersed in the dizzying cacophony of rival artistic styles, persuasions, and theories, he educated himself and found his own direction.

At first Kuniyoshi went from art school to art school, working at menial jobs to support himself. He studied briefly with the charismatic realist painter Robert Henri and the modernist Homer Boss, who had exhibited in the sensational Armory Show. Kuniyoshi was working in a hotel in upstate New York at the time and apparently did not see the Armory Show, but he certainly heard about it, and he knew fellow students like Stuart Davis who exhibited in its American section.

Though still working to master the difficult English language, the quiet, slender immigrant, refined and stylish in his Western clothes, was making friends. He became part of the modern art scene, where artists from diverse but overlapping groups, representing a variety of artistic ideologies, all knew each other. In 1916, settling on the Art Students League as his school, Kuniyoshi discovered an educational environment where he felt at ease and

FIG. 1
Kenneth Hayes Miller, *Landscape with Figures*, c. 1914,
oil on canvas, 20 x 17 in. (50.8 x 43.2 cm), The Metropolitan
Museum of Art, New York

things in depth, one behind another."[4] At the League
Kuniyoshi also met his future wife, Katherine Schmidt,
who later wrote that Miller "opened his [Kuniyoshi's]
heart and eyes to the physical nature and sensuous beauty
of the art of painting."[5]

Today Miller is best known for his paintings of
statuesque women shopping on Fourteenth Street in
Manhattan. In these peculiar, somewhat stilted works
he tried to fuse contemporary subject matter with the
perspective, chiaroscuro, and classical composition he so
admired in Italian Renaissance art. But this was a style
he did not develop until the 1920s. Earlier, when
Kuniyoshi was studying with him, Miller was working
in an American Symbolist mode. Inspired by Albert
Pinkham Ryder, the great American mystical painter
whom he befriended in Ryder's old age, Miller painted
timeless figures in generalized, evocative landscapes,
such as *Landscape with Figures* (c. 1914, fig. 1).

In 1917 Kuniyoshi showed two paintings at the
debut exhibition of the Society of Independent Artists.
One of these works, *Modern Crucifix* (recently rediscov-
ered and now known as *Crucifixion*, fig. 2), gives a sense
of the talented young student striving to assimilate the
European artistic tradition under Miller's tutelage. In his
painting, Kuniyoshi adopted Miller's low horizon and
rolling hills, which helped to silhouette the crucifix tilted
dramatically against the sky. The humble figures at the
base of the cross, which also occur in Kuniyoshi's etchings
from the teens, reflect his teacher's enthusiasm for the
nineteenth-century French realist Honoré Daumier, as
well as the figures of workers in a few of Miller's works in
this period.[6] In adopting one of the most exalted images
of the Christian tradition, Kuniyoshi was working to
incorporate western subject matter as well as style into his
art. Still he managed to create a personal scene, a depar-
ture from the traditional iconography of the Crucifixion:
in his rendering, crouching workers huddle in a vast,
barren landscape beneath a diminutive image of Christ.

The Society of Independent Artists exhibition where
Kuniyoshi showed *Modern Crucifix* was a challenge to the
conservative, juried shows run by the prestigious National
Academy of Design. As a democratic experiment, the
progressive Society of Independent Artists organized a

found companions who would remain close for the rest
of his life. He later wrote: "I had a great hunger for
friends and companionship as a natural reaction from
my lonely wanderings. At the League I found warmth
and kindness which I sorely needed."[2] One of the young
artists he met, Alexander Brook, reminisced: "It must
have been one of us who, recognizing Yas's singular talent,
made the first move, for he was a shy young man. . . .
There was no question in our minds that we wanted
to accept Yas as the latest of kin to the little band of
advanced thinkers and potential artistic innovators that
we fancied ourselves to be."[3]

With a scholarship that gave him financial aid in
exchange for work, Kuniyoshi studied at the league until
1920. In those years he had only one instructor, Kenneth
Hayes Miller—a highly respected teacher whose students
included George Bellows, Edward Hopper, and many
other leading American painters. Miller impressed his
pupils with the seriousness of his dedication to painting
and communicated to them his deep enthusiasm for the
Old Masters. Although Kuniyoshi's fellow students were
very aware of modernism, they mostly admired the pre-
cursors of the latest avant-garde, Renoir and Cézanne,
and for the most part Miller's students developed into
representational painters. Lloyd Goodrich, who would
become an eminent historian of American art, was in
Kuniyoshi's class. When Goodrich interviewed Kuniyoshi
about his career in 1948, the artist remembered that
"when he first came to this country he had been brought
up seeing and feeling things in the oriental way, that is in
a two-dimensional way. . . . Then Miller taught him to see

FIG. 2
Yasuo Kuniyoshi, *Crucifixion*, 1917, oil on canvas, 19 x 24 in.
(48.3 x 61 cm), Collection of Mr. Masatoshi Nakatani,
courtesy of FM Gallery, Tokyo

radical, non-juried exhibition open to any artist who
wanted to submit work. The result was huge, diverse,
stimulating, and chaotic. Many of the offerings were
traditional realist paintings that would have been at
home at the National Academy and that make Kuniyoshi's painting look modern in its simplification of
detail. On the other hand, today this show is best known
for its rejection of Marcel Duchamp's subversive sub-
mission of a urinal that he titled *Fountain* and entered
under a false name. Despite Duchamp's exclusion,
examples of extreme avant-garde art were present in the
show, including Constantin Brancusi's bronze *Princess*,
an almost totally abstract Cubist *Figure* by Picasso, and
non-representational images by Americans such as
Arthur Dove, Georgia O'Keeffe, and Joseph Stella.

The Independents' exhibition was one phenomenon
in the liberalization of the New York art scene in the years
following the mind-expanding Armory Show. The influx
of modernist artists from Europe, who were distancing
themselves from the battlefields of World War I, contributed to this vitality. Another manifestation of this new
energy was the Penguin,[7] a loose organization of progressive artists spearheaded by Walt Kuhn, one of three
organizers of the Armory Show. The Penguins held art
exhibitions and figure drawing sessions in their Greenwich Village headquarters at 8 East 15th Street, as well as
boisterous annual costume parties. Kuniyoshi's drawings
and etchings were included in several of their earliest
shows, which began in 1917. This marked his coming
of age in the New York art world, as he later wrote:

> I was terribly excited to be asked to show my work
> there along with such artists as Kuhn, Weber, Pascin
> and several other noteworthy painters. This small
> but fertile group helped to establish the roots of
> contemporary American painting. Considered rebels
> of their time they waged a vigorous battle against
> conservatism with might and humor.[8]

Key members of the Penguin included French-born
Louis Bouché, who introduced Kuniyoshi and Alexander
Brook to the group, and Wood Gaylor, who documented
many of the club's activities in his brightly colored, folk-
influenced paintings. Another active participant was

Jules Pascin, a Rumanian who had attained celebrity as an
artist in Paris before moving to New York in 1914. The
party-loving Pascin, who stayed in New York until 1920,
developed a coterie of American painters during the years
he lived in Brooklyn Heights, in the same building as
Kuniyoshi. Another dynamic member of the Penguins
was artist Horace Brodzky, an Australian who had moved
to London and befriended Henri Gaudier-Brzeska and
Ezra Pound before spending most of the years between
1906 and 1923 in New York. Brodzky edited and
published several magazines—*Playboy*, *The Quill*, and
Rainbow—covering the arts in Greenwich Village. He
also used his London connections to organize a huge
show of Vorticism, the British equivalent of Futurism,
at the Penguin in 1917.

Probably the last activity of the Penguins was the
Fireman's Dinner in honor of Brancusi when the sculptor
visited in 1926.[9] The artists dressed up like firemen and
decorated the hall with portraits of firefighters. The event
was recorded in a cheerful painting by Alexander Calder
(1926, fig. 3), which showed Bouché at the right, arguing
with some of the rowdier guests, while immediately next
to him a bespectacled Kuniyoshi looks on bemusedly.
Calder's painting was executed in the flattened representational style practiced by many of the Penguin artists at
the time, with recognizable figures and portraits but few
realistic details. Modern in its simplification but still
dedicated to figuration, this broad and flexible style
allowed for a wide variety of personal inflections and
was adopted in various ways by Kuniyoshi himself and
by many of his friends.

Kuniyoshi's participation in the 1917 Independents
exhibition was auspicious because there he met Hamilton
Easter Field. This wealthy man about the arts would soon
furnish Kuniyoshi and his wife with living and working
quarters, during the winters in a building he owned in
Brooklyn Heights and during the summers in his art

FIG. 3
Alexander Calder, *Fireman's Dinner for Brancusi*, 1926,
oil on canvas, 36 x 42 in. (91.4 x 106.7 cm), Whitney Museum
of American Art, New York, gift of the artist

Art colonies flourished in the United States at the turn of the century in places like Old Lyme, Connecticut, and Provincetown, Massachusetts.[11] Following the example of European groups like the French Barbizon painters, the Impressionists, or Gauguin and his followers in Brittany, artists would find beautiful, unspoiled locales and summer there, painting and often teaching art and encouraging other artists to join them. Kuniyoshi spent summers in congenial art colonies for most of his career. In the summer of 1918, he lived in Woodstock, New York, one of the most popular art colonies in the United States, while attending the Art Students League Summer School. After several summers in Ogunquit, in 1929 he and Katherine Schmidt bought land and built a house in Woodstock, which would be his summer residence for the rest of his life.

colony in Ogunquit, Maine. Field would also play a significant role in the formation of Kuniyoshi's aesthetic. A man of many accomplishments, Field was active as an art critic, painter, dealer, teacher, and collector. Generous and idealistic, he spent part of his inherited fortune helping many artists he believed in, including Marsden Hartley, Maurice Sterne, and Max Weber. Field had studied art in Paris with Jean-Léon Gérôme and Henri Fantin-Latour, and most of his paintings were landscapes or interiors in a conservative, pre-Impressionist style. But he made occasional forays into modernism, and as a critic and entrepreneur he supported advanced trends. He constantly stressed the importance of originality, of the artist finding his own voice. With typical boldness, in 1909 he commissioned Picasso to paint a series of Cubist murals for his mother's house in Brooklyn Heights.[10] In 1911 he and his protégé, Robert Laurent, founded the Thurnscoe School of Modern Art in Ogunquit, where Kuniyoshi would spend productive summers in the late teens and early twenties.

Field first visited Ogunquit in 1902 with twelve-year-old Robert Laurent, the future sculptor he had met in France and brought to New York with his parents. Field, who eventually would make Laurent his heir, took him north to look for a summer residence where they could escape the city's heat. Impressed by the beauty of the little fishing village and its similarity to Laurent's native Brittany, Field bought property in Ogunquit. They were not the first artists to discover the place: Boston-based Charles Woodbury had been visiting since 1888 and had established a summer art school in 1898.[12] Woodbury's house and studio stood overlooking the ocean on one side of a little inlet, Perkins Cove. Field bought up a group of fishermen's shacks on the other side of the cove and remodeled the main residence on the promontory, with its wonderful view of the ocean. The imposing houses of the two art school masters confronted each other across a narrow strip of water; Field represented the modernist persuasion, while Woodbury stood for the traditional. An early photograph of the fishermen's huts on Perkins Cove shows the sort of shack that Field provided for Kuniyoshi and Katherine Schmidt (fig. 4). Woodbury's painting of Field's Island House (1910, fig. 5) conveys the majestic setting of the building and also serves as a good example of Woodbury's style. A former engineering student at MIT, he was fascinated with the movement of waves, which were his most

FIG. 4
Robert Laurent's papers included this photograph of Perkins Cove, Ogunquit, Maine, c.1911, gelatin silver print, 5¾ x 2¾ in. (14.6 x 7 cm), photograph courtesy of Paul Laurent

FIG. 5
Charles H. Woodbury N.A., *The Island House*, 1910, oil on canvas, 20 x 30 in. (50.8 x 76.2 cm),
signed lower right and left, owned by Ruth R. Woodbury

frequent subject. Here he painted them with a lush and luminous Impressionist palette and creamy brushstrokes, both spontaneous and controlled, reminiscent of the style of his good friend, John Singer Sargent.

A Kuniyoshi landscape from his first summer in Maine is also painterly, but where Woodbury portrayed a specific house, and virtually a specific wave, Kuniyoshi's *Thurnscoe, Maine* is much more generalized (1918, fig. 6). Moody and dark, with a deliberate eschewal of bright color, it recalls Ryder's and Miller's interiorized, subjective landscapes and gives little foreshadowing of the stark, individualistic paintings, such as *Maine Family* (1922-23, pl. 4), that Kuniyoshi would create a few years later.

In Ogunquit Kuniyoshi married Katherine Schmidt in 1919, when she was twenty-one years old and he had just turned thirty. Hamilton Easter Field presided at the wedding, and among the guests were artist friends from the Maine summer colony, including Robert Laurent and his French bride Mimi, Niles and Betty Spencer, and probably Bernard Karfiol, Dorothy Varian, Stefan Hirsch, caricaturist Isabella Howland, and cartoonist Edmund Duffy.[13] The wedding had its own drama because the bride's family, who resolutely opposed the marriage, cut her off financially and did not speak to her for six years.[14] Due to American law, Schmidt also lost her United States

citizenship by marrying a Japanese citizen. It was a torturous time for Kuniyoshi, and the debate about the marriage extended to the Art Students League, according to classmate Arnold Blanch: "Some of his friends didn't think it was the right thing for a Japanese to marry an

FIG. 6
Yasuo Kuniyoshi, *Thurnscoe, Maine*, 1918, oil on canvas, mounted on board, 8¼ x 10⁵⁄₁₆ in. (21 x 26.2 cm), Fujikawa Galleries, Inc., Tokyo, photograph courtesy of Michael Owen Gallery, New York

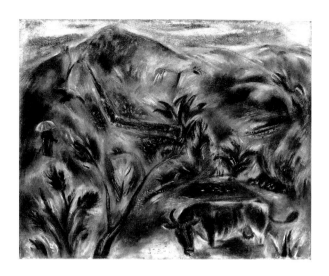

American girl, and so forth and so on. There were some for him and some against him and it got to be a great controversy amongst the students."[15]

Once married, the couple faced a financial struggle, and Field's help was sometimes unreliable. Kuniyoshi had occasionally sold drawings and small paintings at moderate prices to friends and fellow students; in fact, he paid some of the wedding expenses in this fashion. After the wedding he continued doing odd jobs for Field, and his wife took the demanding position of running the dining room of the Art Students League. In addition, Kuniyoshi turned to photography, as documented in his 1924 *Self-Portrait* (pl. 12). In his own words: "I bought a regular studio camera and practiced taking pictures by using my own canvases as models. Photography agreed with me for I learned quickly and in between painting I received commissions from friends and galleries for photographing sculpture and paintings. The winters were spent in this fashion and in the summers I devoted my time to painting in Ogunquit."[16] Alexander Brook saw a downside: "Going from place to place lugging his camera and other necessary photographic paraphernalia consumed too much of Yas's time and energy."[17] But despite the lack of material comforts, the combination of married life, winters in New York, and summers in Ogunquit was good for Kuniyoshi's art. In 1920 Charles Daniel began showing his work at his Daniel Gallery, one of the few places in New York that exhibited contemporary art. In 1921 Kuniyoshi started making works—including his distinctive black-and-white pen and brush drawings—that established him as a truly original artist.

Kuniyoshi showed two paintings at Daniel's in 1920, in a group show that included prominent artists like William Glackens, Robert Henri, and Maurice Prendergast, as well as newcomers like Thomas Hart Benton, Charles Demuth, Marsden Hartley, Man Ray, and Charles Sheeler.[18] *Landscape* (c. 1920, fig. 7) could have been one of the paintings in the show. In it the artist moved toward his new style, with a bucolic subject and earthy palette. Rejecting Miller's Renaissance-inspired concept of "things in space, one behind the other," Kuniyoshi instead substituted a flattened space with a big cow cropped off at the lower right and an absurd

little figure under an umbrella floating in the left middle ground. With its elements of modernism, Japanese art, and American folk painting, *Landscape* announces the unique style that would solidify in Kuniyoshi's art in 1921.

Kuniyoshi had his first one-man show with Daniel in early 1922. *Boy Frightened by Snake* (1921, fig. 8) typifies the eccentricity of some of the paintings he showed that year. Composed like a secular Crucifixion, it is flat and centralized but at the same time languorously active with its pinwheel format and graceful curves. The tiny snake occupies an irrational spatial hole in the two-dimensional scene, while the lake behind the boy arches over his head like a frame. Kuniyoshi acknowledged being influenced by German Expressionists in these years, specifically two artists affiliated with Der Blaue Reiter group, Heinrich Campendonk and Albert Bloch; Daniel had shown the latter's paintings in the exhibition previous to Kuniyoshi's.[19] Some of his rejection of traditional space and his freedom to distort the figure was encouraged by their work, and by European modernism in general. But the strange psychology of *Boy Frightened by Snake* is peculiar to Kuniyoshi. The boy's passive face lends an unexpected mood to the emotion of fear, which is communicated primarily by the title. Although many works in the history of art include frightened figures as part of their imagery, it is very unusual for an artist to make the emotion of fear a work's primary subject. Yet Kuniyoshi did so repeatedly. In *Boy Frightened by Lightning* (1921, fig. 9), a pen and brush drawing also in the 1922 Daniel show, a boy expresses his anxiety more visibly, sitting with his knees to his chest, covering his ears and closing his eyes. A contemporary reviewer wrote that "the figure, without melodramatic posing, is composed so as to give the impression of some one stunned by momentary fear" and concluded, "Yasuo Kuniyoshi has a good start toward greatness."[20]

FIG. 8
Yasuo Kuniyoshi, *Boy Frightened by Snake*, 1921, oil on canvas, 24 x 20 in. (61 x 50.8 cm), location unknown, photograph courtesy of Whitney Museum of American Art, New York, Library, Kuniyoshi files

toys, and textiles. Marsden Hartley painted comparable centralized compositions, such as *Vase of Flowers* (fig. 10), while residing in Field's colony in Ogunquit in 1917. Hartley further emulated local traditions by painting his symmetrical arrangements on the backs of pieces of glass, a long-established folk practice.[21] On the other hand, Kuniyoshi's quickly brushed drawing, executed in deep black ink, somewhat recalls the sumi ink brush traditions of his native country. By painting the background black and leaving the edge of the field ragged and gestural, he also drew attention to the medium itself—the ink represents dark, empty space but simultaneously asserts itself as nothing more than ink, establishing a paradox that is crucial to modernist painting.

Boy Frightened by Lightning features a youthful protagonist, as do many of Kuniyoshi's works of this period. In *Baby and Toy Cow* (1921, pl. 22), a serious baby with a distended head floats at the top of the scene, crawling towards a toy boat, a toy cow, and a toy decorated with a yin-yang image. He inches across a blanket covered with landscape images that would recur frequently in Kuniyoshi's art of the next few years, including the leafless tree, barren and wistful. Their appearance on a cloth suggests that the distinctive decorative qualities found in the artist's later landscapes have a source in his early training in textile design before he left Japan. Kuniyoshi painted parts of this drawing, such as the flanks of the cow and its wheels, with dense black ink and then scratched through it with a pointed tool to create torn white highlights. This is a distinctive technique he employed in many of his drawings to heighten the expressiveness of the rich physical surfaces. The drawing also exemplifies the artist's taste for images that do not totally fill the frame of the page, again subverting Renaissance compositional practices.

With *Eggplant* (1921, pl. 21), a still life of beautiful simplicity, Kuniyoshi began an exploration of still-life subjects that he continued in a series of ink drawings during the 1920s. Its symmetry echoes the still lifes of American folk art painters at a time when American artists were just beginning to appreciate such works. Hamilton Easter Field wrote about American folk arts and crafts, and he and his artist friends in Ogunquit were early collectors of folk paintings, furniture, ceramics,

FIG. 9
Yasuo Kuniyoshi, *Boy Frightened by Lightning*, 1921, pen and ink, brush and ink on paper, 20 x 16 in. (50.8 x 40.6 cm), location unknown, photograph courtesy of Whitney Museum of American Art, New York, Library, Kuniyoshi files

FIG. 10
Marsden Hartley, *Vase of Flowers*, 1917, oil on glass, 13¼ x 8⅞ in. (33.7 x 22.4 cm), Fisk University, Nashville, Tennessee, The Alfred Stieglitz Collection of Modern Art

original."[25] His praise was in harmony with other critics, led by Hamilton Easter Field, who were impressed with Kuniyoshi's originality.

Kuniyoshi's development in the early 1920s compares with that of Niles Spencer, a fellow painter in Ogunquit, who experienced a similar firming up of his style at around the same time. Spencer, encouraged by the sharp edges he was seeing in American folk paintings and in the landscape itself, with its geometrical fisherman's shacks, moved from his more loosely painted earlier work towards the hard-edged forms that would make him a leading exemplar of the American Precisionist style. Spencer's *The Cove* (1922, fig. 11) is anchored in perceivable reality, recording the view from the window at his studio on Perkins Cove. Anticipating the industrial forms that would become the focus of his art, Spencer's painting depicts two peninsulas jutting out into the water, into traditional illusionistic space. Kuniyoshi also moved from the softly brushed, Renoiresque contours of earlier landscapes like *Thurnscoe* (see fig. 6). His *Adam and Eve (The Fall of Man)* (1922, pl. 1) interprets a traditional Christian theme in his own vocabulary, with a palette dominated by deep greens and earth colors and a space

The reviews of Kuniyoshi's first one-man show raised an issue central to his career, as some critics attempted to explain his art's strangeness by reference to his Asian heritage—with mixed results. A critic for the *New York Times* wrote: "In the artist's unerring registry of the emotion of fright, we have once more the genius of his artistically expressive race,"[22] while another articulated a different stereotype, criticizing the drawing *Cock and Snake* for being overly influenced by the "aloofness of Eastern art."[23] A writer in the *World* developed a more insightful analysis: "With true Asiatic subtlety, and at the same time in perfectly frank and guileless sincerity, he has applied the dynamics of 'cubism' to the flat perspective and synthetic abstractions of Oriental drawing."[24]

This discussion was continued by William Murrell, who wrote the introduction to a small monograph devoted to Kuniyoshi's work. Published in Woodstock as part of a Younger Artist series, the pamphlet reproduced most of the works from the artist's first Daniel Gallery show. In his text Murrell distinguished Kuniyoshi from the majority of Japanese artists who emigrated to the United States and "swallowed Western technique whole. . . . Yasuo Kuniyoshi is perhaps the only Japanese now painting in America whose work is free from both Oriental and Occidental academic influences as such; the single instance of a selective blending of dynamic elements from two great traditions into a style distinctly

FIG. 11
Niles Spencer, *The Cove*, 1922, oil on canvas, 28 x 36 in. (71.1 x 91.4 cm), Collection of the Newark Museum, New Jersey, purchase 1926

that is curiously upturned. An eccentric pond rises up to frame Adam with its irregular halo. The stocky first couple interacts with a sort of mock solemnity in a landscape teeming with animal and botanical life, while a two-headed snake, with both tongues thrust out, slithers across a jagged, angular rock formation, orchestrating the temptation.

Like most of Kuniyoshi's major paintings, in *Adam and Eve* the artist jotted down his main idea with a quick graphite sketch, then made it monumental and concrete on the canvas (1922, fig. 12). In this casual drawing the artist comfortably adopted a floating, unphotographic space. The people, plants, and animals that populate it would be the dominant subjects of his entire oeuvre, again in contrast to his friend Spencer, whose work would emphasize industrial imagery.

Kuniyoshi's familiarity with a wide variety of animals and insects dates back to his youth. His family's modest home was only a few blocks from Koraku-en Park in Okayama. There he could have seen many of the creatures that populate the Eden in *Adam and Eve (The Fall of Man)*, from the grasshopper at Eve's feet to the catfish Adam is absent-mindedly holding. A frog floats next to him, while a rooster dives crazily from the sky. To the right of Eve a cow serenely excretes—a strangely proportioned cow, with a bulky, angular body and a wedge-shaped head. Its humanized eye and calm gaze give it an aura of wisdom at odds with the fact that cows are relatively unintelligent mammals, and a gentle humor results from the contrast of opposites. This peculiar type of cow became one of Kuniyoshi's trademarks, and its relatives would dominate his second exhibition at Daniel's, held at the beginning of 1923.

When asked why he was so fascinated with cows, Kuniyoshi would answer that by the Japanese calendar he was born in a cow year. To his American questioners, his reply emphasized his exoticism: "According to legend I believed my fate to be guided, more or less, by the bovine kingdom."[26] At the same time, cows were rare in Japan

and fascinatingly strange to the young immigrant painter.[27] In the words of critic Henry McBride, a consistent supporter of Kuniyoshi's work: "This Japanese, in spite of his early advent to these shores, is still a Japanese, and sees things in the civilization that we have arranged much as an arrival from Mars might."[28]

That Kuniyoshi deliberately moved his art towards greater distortion starting in 1921 is evident from comparing the more normally proportioned cow in his early *Landscape* (see fig. 7) with *The Calf Doesn't Want to Go* (1922, pl. 24) from his 1923 Daniel show. Even though the second cow is oddly configured, its body language is understood as it stiffens its legs and leans back in resistance to the farm boy's pressure. Boy and calf are almost equal in size, and the contrast between his blank expression and the animal's wise stare out at the viewer makes their contest one between equals. It is a timeless standoff, a humorous American version of bucolic themes that go back to Roman antiquity.

While this scene and others like *Three Cows and One Calf* (1922, pl. 23) were rooted in the artist's experience of Maine farm life, the cow that pokes its thoughtful head into *The Dream* (1922, pl. 29) takes part in a proto-Surrealist fantasy. In a horizonless space a young girl levitates with a bird, above a snake-infested tree stump and below a whirling eclipse. *The Dream* was in Kuniyoshi's 1923 Daniel exhibition, along with a companion painting titled *Dream* (1922, pl. 2). These works present another side of Kuniyoshi's art, stressing the irrational and the psychological, that led Henry McBride to compare him with such masters of imagination as William Blake and Odilon Redon.[29]

At the beginning of 1924, Daniel continued his practice of giving Kuniyoshi a New Year's exhibition that summed up his work from the preceding year. The show was well received by critics, who were impressed by the artist's originality and sense of humor. Kuniyoshi, one felt, "evinces the peculiar detachment of the Oriental."[30] The critics especially praised his black and white drawings, which several observers related to Japanese ink brush paintings, while one commented: "In them too is a curious Japanese angle of vision, for Mr. Kuniyoshi, in taking up Western materials, has remained true to

FIG. 13
Bernard Karfiol, *Virginie Combing Her Hair*, 1922,
oil on canvas, 18 x 30 in. (45.7 x 76.2 cm), Ogunquit
Museum of American Art, Ogunquit, Maine

Brook, and Bouché, as well as the sculptors Gaston
Lachaise and Elie Nadelman. This was also true of the
Ogunquit group, which featured some of the same people
as well as Robert Laurent, Leon Kroll, and Bernard
Karfiol. Karfiol's 1922 painting titled *Virginie Combing
Her Hair* (fig. 13) exemplifies the realism, simplified
in response to modernism but still quite traditional,
practiced by many of these men. Karfiol had studied
in Paris and had met Picasso, Gertrude Stein, and other
members of the Paris avant-garde before returning to the
United States in 1906 and becoming another of the
artists helped by Field. His art was esteemed in its time
for its "sensitivity," but today this painting seems weakly
classicizing with its profile head and slender anatomy,
whereas Kuniyoshi's *After the Bath* has a robust eccentric-

FIG. 14
Yasuo Kuniyoshi, *Child*, 1923, oil on canvas, 30 x 24 in.
(76.2 x 61 cm), Whitney Museum of American Art, New York,
gift of Mrs. Edith Gregor Halpert

his Oriental blood. His art could not come from a
Western mind."[31]

Kuniyoshi showed some wonderful drawings in this
exhibition. In them he introduced lush gray shadows,
made with ink wash often reinforced with graphite, which
invest the objects with a sensuous three-dimensionality
that plays against the warped perspective he simultaneously created. *Grapes in White Bowl* (1923, pl. 14)
continues the centralized composition of *Eggplant*
(pl. 21) but sets the voluptuously rounded bowl against
a flat white space. In *Dish with Banana* (1923, pl. 16),
Kuniyoshi added a touch of color to his ink and graphite
combination to heighten the delicate eroticism of his
still life of an oval fruit dish with a pale yellow banana
inserted into it, "trying unsuccessfully to look innocent,"
according to a contemporary reviewer.[32]

A greater sexuality is also evident in *After the Bath*
(1923, pl. 7). Originally titled *Captain's Daughter*, this
painting shown at the Daniel Gallery depicts a half-nude
young woman combing her hair. Female nudes were
common subjects among Kuniyoshi's male artist friends
who congregated at the Penguin, including Kuhn, Pascin,

ity in details like the minutely drawn strands of hair and their contrast with the bather's bulky arms.[33] The boat outside the window was interpreted at the time as belonging to her seafaring father, who has left her at home to comb her hair. The suggestive object next to her is a curling iron—an object rare in Japan, which Kuniyoshi painted with fascinated precision.

With *Boy Stealing Fruit* (1923, pl. 5), Kuniyoshi again showed his ability to invent unusual and psychologically loaded subjects. Originally titled *Boy Stealing Forbidden Fruit*, it is a secular *Fall of Man* with no Eve necessary to convince this guilty little Adam to yield to temptation.[34] Kuniyoshi's unique combination of volumetric modeling with warped perspectives, plus his exaggeration of the youth's stoutness and his insight

FIG. 15
John Bradley, *Little Girl in Lavender*, c. 1840, oil on canvas, 33¾ x 27⁵⁄₁₆ in. (85.7 x 69.4 cm), National Gallery of Art, Washington, D.C., gift of Edgar William and Bernice Chrysler Garbish

into a furtive moment, make this an unforgettable painting. His interest in children is continued in *Child* (1923, fig. 14), where a toddler poses formally, with a military uprightness. The boy's precocious maturity was indicated more fully in the painting's original title, *The Einstein Child*.[35] Kuniyoshi's artistic fascination with young children is characteristic, and it suggests that he had some sort of identification with them. Certainly the combination of naiveté and maturity of *Child*, the sense of sophistication coupled with disingenuousness, is found in much of Kuniyoshi's art in this period.

A similar feeling was also present in eighteenth- and nineteenth-century American folk art, which included many examples of children formally standing for their portraits (fig. 15).[36] In another instance of the artist responding to folk imagery, the birds in Kuniyoshi's *Boy Feeding Chickens* (1923, fig. 16), depicted in profile, emulate American weather vanes (fig. 17). His enthusiasm was carried into an exhibition he curated at the Whitney Studio Club, the forerunner of the Whitney Museum of American Art, in April 1924. By this time Kuniyoshi was respected in the New York art world. His annual exhibitions at the Daniel Gallery were well received, and since 1922 he had been a director of the Salons of America, the exhibition group founded by Field in competition with the Independents. He also was active in the Penguin and the Whitney Studio Club, and he and Katherine had a large and active group of artist friends. When Juliana Force, director of the Whitney Studio Club, decided to hold a group of exhibitions curated by artists in 1924, he was a logical choice. Kuniyoshi's was the last in the series, which included two shows of contemporary American art, one organized by cartoonist W. E. Hill and the other by John Sloan. Alexander Brook selected works by two Mexican artists, José Clemente Orozco and Miguel Covarrubias, and juxtaposed them with paintings by the nineteenth-century American E. L. Henry. Henry Schnakenberg's "Early American Art" show, "the first public exhibition of American folk art,"[37] featured paintings and objects borrowed from his artist friends, including Charles Demuth, Charles Sheeler, Katherine Schmidt, and Kuniyoshi. The latter loaned a

FIG. 16
Yasuo Kuniyoshi, *Boy Feeding Chickens*, 1923, oil on canvas,
29 x 23 in. (73.7 x 58.4 cm), The National Museum of
Modern Art, Kyoto

painting of a locomotive seen in rigid profile, along with
a carved wooden cow.[38]

Sheeler curated the show just before Kuniyoshi's,
featuring works by George Braque, Duchamp, Picasso,
and Marius de Zayas. Kuniyoshi's exhibition, titled
"Portraits and Religious Works," presented religious
pieces by John Mauro, a visionary painter from Patterson,
New Jersey, who contributed a huge *Crucifixion* and other
spiritual scenes, probably including the strange symbolic
scene on the cover of the exhibition's catalogue.[39] Supple-
menting these works was a large assembly of portraits,
some by French modernists such as Matisse and Raoul
Dufy but most by Kuniyoshi's friends and colleagues,
including George Ault, Louis Eilshemius, Karfiol, Kuhn,
Reginald Marsh, Waldo Pierce, Spencer, and Joseph
Stella. Critics praised the show's liveliness, as Kuniyoshi
brought together American outsider art, Parisian modernism (in its less abstract manifestations), and progressive
American contemporary art—some of the most potent
tendencies swirling around the New York art world in the
early 1920s.

Kuniyoshi's own style, like that of his colleagues in
Ogunquit and in the Penguin, constituted a conservative
modernism as opposed to academic realism, incorporating
elements of abstraction but remaining rooted in represen-
tation. This was evident in the works from 1924 that he
showed at Daniel's at the end of the year. *Baby Frightened
by Water* continued the artist's personal concerns with
infancy and with fear, but many paintings in the show
featured stocky, powerful women bathers, following the

idiosyncratic eroticism already seen in *After the Bath*
(pl. 7). In *Bather with Cigarette* (1924, pl. 10), a bulky
Venus with bulging face and body holds her cigarette
between the tips of two fingers in a gesture that is both
incongruously dainty and slightly rebellious, since it was
then a liberated act for women to smoke in public. The
bather takes a dip in Kuniyoshi's *The Swimmer* (1924,
pl. 11), where her feminine rotundities are contrasted
with the angular and erect forms of the island and the
lighthouse that float above her. The painting makes a
revealing comparison with *Lighthouse Hill* (1927, fig. 18)
by Edward Hopper, who visited Ogunquit several times
in the teens. Hopper's painting is the quintessence of the
European realistic tradition, with its consistently representational light, proportion, perspective, and color. All
these are warped and fanciful in Kuniyoshi's painting,
with its buoyant figure and flattened architecture. Hopper's realism characteristically communicates a feeling of
heroic isolation, whereas the lighthouse in Kuniyoshi's
painting—resembling Nubble Light in York, Maine—
seems to accompany and protect the lone swimmer, and
the curtains in the keeper's quarters suggest a comforting
domesticity. Kuniyoshi's *Waitresses from the Sparhawk*
(1924/25, pl. 13) presents the antithesis of Hopper's

FIG. 17
Artist unknown, *Rooster Weathervane*, c. 1825, copper,
33 in. high (83.8 cm), Abby Aldrich Rockefeller Folk Art
Center, Williamsburg, Virginia

FIG. 18
Edward Hopper, *Lighthouse Hill*, 1927, oil on canvas, 28¼ x 39½ in. (71.8 x 100.3 cm), Dallas Museum of Art,
gift of Mr. and Mrs. Maurice Purnell

famous loneliness, as two waitresses from an Ogunquit hotel trip across the Maine landscape, arms linked in a gesture of comfortable camaraderie. Kuniyoshi's *Life Saver* (1924, pl. 9), equally unusual in subject, features perhaps the dullest rainbow ever painted, a testimony to the artist's love of earth colors in these years. The ambiguous relationship of the title to the painting's image, of a man in a sailor cap staring blankly at a bather who preens for him, typifies the strangeness of Kuniyoshi's paintings from the early 1920s. Henry McBride, reviewing Kuniyoshi's 1925 show at Daniel, which featured most of these paintings, attributed this quality to a unique fusion of Japanese sensibilities with American subjects. "The result must be as astonishing to the Japanese who sees this art as it is to us . . . but the time will come, assuredly, when the Japanese will share with us an admiration of this joint product of the two nations."[40]

Many contemporary critics felt that the key to Kuniyoshi's artistic individuality was his Japanese background, and they tried to locate it with moderate success. Finding a better definition of this quality is a key issue in evaluating Kuniyoshi's work and his place in art history, particularly since he himself defined as

his artistic aim "to combine the rich traditions of the East with my accumulative experiences and viewpoint of the West."[41]

During his student years in New York, two influential men deepened Kuniyoshi's appreciation of types of art that would inflect his work: Kenneth Hayes Miller and Hamilton Easter Field. A magnificent drawing like *Squash* (1924, pl. 19) owes its intense roundness to the illusionistic modeling the artist learned from Miller and the latter's enthusiasm for the techniques of the Old Masters. Kuniyoshi chose an indigenous American vegetable as his subject, but his modeling sets the drawing apart from closely related examples of nineteenth-century American folk art (fig. 19). The squash bulges with volume, but the plate is tilted up, flattened out, disobeying the laws of Renaissance perspective. This is a characteristic found in three disparate sources of Kuniyoshi's inspiration—Japanese art, European modernism, and American folk art. In fact, the early modernists, the Impressionists and Post-Impressionists, were directly inspired by Japanese prints. Some later modernists, including the Blaue Reiter artists who influenced Hartley, were encouraged by the absence of perspective in folk art.

FIG. 19
Artist unknown, *Watermelon in Blue Bordered Dish*, c. 1840, watercolor, 11½ x 16¾ in. (29.2 x 42.6 cm), Abby Aldrich Rockefeller Folk Art Center, Williamsburg, Virginia

Thus it is impossible to attribute this flattened perspective to one source or another.

In terms of contemporary art, *Squash* relates to Precisionism through Kuniyoshi's obsessive detailing of every lump and protrusion of the vegetable, and Precisionists like Sheeler and Spencer were also very interested in American folk art. But the warped oval of the plate and the passionately organic quality of every element in the drawing removes it from the orbit of this machine-inspired style. *Squash*'s style is distinctly Kuniyoshi's.

While Miller inspired his students with his enthusiasm for the Old Master tradition, he was less encouraging when it came to Asian art. With his love of Renaissance illusionism, he felt that the highest achievement of painting was "the fullest embodiment of expression in three-dimensional substance," further noting that "[i]n the East this step was never taken."[42] But Field was a mentor of a different sort. During his lifetime he was considered one of the leading experts on Japanese art in the United States, and he actively encouraged Kuniyoshi to retain aspects of his Japanese artistic heritage in his work. Field's interest in Japanese art had flourished in Paris, where he studied for over a decade starting in 1894.[43] In Paris he was hosted by relatives, including members of the Haviland family, whose china company pioneered the appropriation of Japanese motifs in the late nineteenth century. Charles Haviland had married the daughter of Philippe Burty, the art critic who coined the term "japonisme" and who, with Manet, Degas, and other friends, was an early appreciator of Japanese art. With the guidance of his family, Field built an important collection of Japanese prints that he brought back to the United States from Paris.

In 1920 Field founded *The Arts* magazine, and until his death from pneumonia in 1922—when he was only forty-six—Field saw to it that this magazine, primarily dedicated to contemporary art, featured an article on Japanese art in every issue. His ideas were more broad-minded and ecumenical than Miller's. Of Leonardo da Vinci's statements on art, Field wrote:

> Leonardo's outlook on art is thoroughly Florentine and is therefore tinged with a certain provincialism. It would have been impossible for Leonardo to admit that there could be an art ignoring chiaroscuro and perspective yet of tremendous import. . . . Knowing nothing of the abstract art of the Orient, he could conceive of no great painting devoid of these essentially Western attributes.[44]

In Kuniyoshi Field saw an ideal fusion of Asian and Western cultures. His 1922 review of Kuniyoshi's first exhibition at Daniel's praised his work, in contrast to paintings by other Japanese artists then working in New York: "He has expressed the ideals of modern Japan and of modern America as he has read them fused together in his own heart. He has used an alien technique as if it were his native language. . . . He is, so far as I know, the first modern Japanese who in art has given us a message which, for us Occidentals, has unity, truth and intensity."[45]

One of the painters Field contrasted with Kuniyoshi was the now-forgotten Kyohei Inukai, who was born in Okayama three years before Kuniyoshi and who had studied painting in San Francisco and Chicago before moving to New York and becoming a fashionable portraitist. In a review from 1921, Field criticized Inukai's art in terms that might well have been inspirational to Kuniyoshi: "I believe that, if Kyohei Inukai were to steep himself in the Japanese tradition without abandoning the technique which he has learned of us, he would do work of far greater interest than anything which he might do built entirely on western models."[46]

A comparison of self-portraits by both artists gives some sense of what Field meant. In his *Reflection* of 1918 (fig. 20), Inukai depicted his body in elegant profile, in a room that is illusionistically defined by overlapping perspectival objects, including his palette and a piano. As a visual pun, he depicts the painting itself leaning into the scene at the right edge, while the artist clutches a paint rag and turns his head to look dramatically out at the viewer. In contrast, Kuniyoshi presented himself much less gracefully in his 1924 *Self-Portrait as a Photographer*

FIG. 20
Kyohei Inukai, *Reflection [Self-Portrait]*, 1918, oil on canvas, The National Museum of Modern Art, Tokyo

Kuniyoshi's drawing *Bad Dream* (1924, pl. 30) depicts three women being tormented by monsters and metamorphic creatures; the serene imagery of his painting and drawing *The Dream* (pls. 2 and 29) from two years before has become malevolent. The drawing's black ink and its floating space can be related to Japanese art, and in this case Kuniyoshi was unusually explicit, depicting two well-known Japanese deities in the scene: Shinrai, the Thunder God, with his great arc of drums, at the top left and Tatsumi Kaze, the Wind God, at the far right.[48] Both have been frequently illustrated by Japanese artists, usually as a pair, as in a painting titled *Shinrai* (fig. 21) by Ogata Korin, an artist Kuniyoshi particularly admired.[49] However, the woman being dragged off by a demon at the bottom of *Bad Dream* derives from Western scenes of the Last Judgment, so that the very imagery of the drawing fuses the two traditions.

Kuniyoshi's references to Japanese culture generally were not as literal as they are in *Bad Dream*, and additional insight into his cross-cultural approach can be gained by looking more closely at Hamilton Easter Field and his beliefs about what art should be. While it is

(pl. 12). His back is to the viewer, so that he must twist his head unnaturally to look over his shoulder. His right hand is raised above his head, pointing forward with an awkward and inexplicable gesture. Where Inukai showed himself with artistic long hair, Kuniyoshi's head is covered with a black shroud, which looks both ridiculous and ritualistic. The ritual in which he is engaged is the modern one of taking a photograph; instead of Inukai's traditional paint rag, Kuniyoshi's hand grasps a shutter bulb.[47]

Kuniyoshi heightened the complexity of this strange painting with a multileveled visual pun. He depicted himself photographing a simplified landscape with a barren tree and a few delicate plants, as seen in his contemporary paintings of Maine. A molding at the bottom separates this view from the room containing the photographer and his camera, but is this molding a window frame or a painting's frame? It is impossible to ascertain whether Kuniyoshi is shown here photographing a landscape or a work of art. But whichever it is, he rendered it in a grisaille that anticipates the black and white of the photograph he is in the process of making. In the end, Kuniyoshi's distorted anatomy, flattened space, and ambiguous imagery are more modern than Inukai's, which evoke Sargent and the tradition of European bravura portraiture.

FIG. 21
Ogata Korin, *Shinrai*, panel from *Wind God and Thunder God*, Edo period, 18th century, Kyoryokukai, Tokyo National Museum, Tokyo, Japan

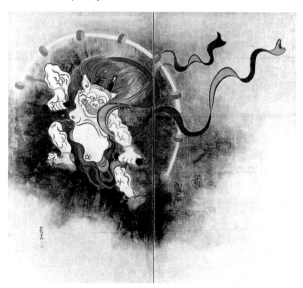

FIG. 22
Utagawa Kuniyoshi, *Crabs*, 1853, 8⁷/₁₆ x 9½ in. (21.4 x 24.2 cm), Museum of Fine Arts, Springfield, Massachusetts, Raymond Bidwell Collection

impossible to know what he and Kuniyoshi talked about at their first meeting at the Independents in 1917, it seems likely that Field would have remarked on the similarity between Kuniyoshi's name and that of one of his favorite *ukiyo-e* printmakers, the nineteenth-century Utagawa Kuniyoshi—particularly since Field had just published an article on him. In this essay Field singled out the print titled *Crab and Rocks at Ebb Tide at Shubi No Matsu* (1853, fig. 22) as

> possibly the most original of all his prints, for in it he has realized a landscape as it would be seen by an inquisitive crustacean. In the foreground an adventurous shrimp has reached the summit of a mountain, in a cleft of a rocky cliff a crab has entrenched himself, while in the distance man and his labors dwindle as, from the crab's point of view, they should.[50]

This unusually low point of view appears frequently in Yasuo Kuniyoshi's work from the early 1920s. In the painting titled *Dream* (pl. 2), for example, the plants at the bottom of the canvas loom larger than the cow, figure, and buildings above them. In the ink drawing *Weeds and Sun* (1923, fig. 23), the enormous plant at the left dwarfs the tiny tree and building at right. Here Kuniyoshi has created a space that is not Cubist and not Expressionist, that perhaps could be related to some folk-influenced modernists like Campendonk, Marc Chagall, and Henri Rousseau. The irrational scale relationships look forward to some Surrealist works. (Surrealism did not yet officially exist, although Jean Miro's paintings from the early twenties manifest a fascination with subhuman life forms parallel to Kuniyoshi's.) Kuniyoshi translated the unusual space from his drawing into painting in *Fish and Seaweed* (1923, pl. 8), where he also echoed the elder Kuniyoshi's interest in marine life.

Fish are known the world over, but in an island nation like Japan they are particularly important to the cuisine and culture. The prevalence of marine animals in Kuniyoshi's work may well have encouraged American critics to feel there was something "Japanese" in his work. True, he was spending his summers in Ogunquit, a fisherman's village, but his American peers who were there

with him, like Karfiol, Kuhn, and Spencer, were content to paint landscapes and figures and were not drawn to unusual subjects like *Fisherman* (1924, pl. 31). At the right in this work, an anthology of sea creatures, including a flounder, an eel, and an octopus, is laid out like a series of biological specimens below the skillful fisherman. This splendid drawing also highlights Kuniyoshi's wonderful sensitivity to the values and textures of black and white, and his peculiar spaces with huge plants towering over figures and animals.

Another oddity by American standards is the prevalence in Kuniyoshi's imagery of the octopus. This is a subject he again shared with his nineteenth-century namesake, whose *Ama Dressing Her Hair on the Sea Shore*

FIG. 23
Yasuo Kuniyoshi, *Weeds and Sun*, 1923, pen and ink, brush and ink on paper, 13½ x 18 in. (34.3 x 45.7 cm), private collection, Japan, courtesy of Gallery Nii, Osaka, photograph courtesy of Whitney Museum of American Art, New York, Library, Kuniyoshi files

FIG. 24
Utagawa Kuniyoshi, *Ama Dressing Her Hair on the Sea Shore*,
c. 1843, wood block print, Victoria and Albert Museum,
London

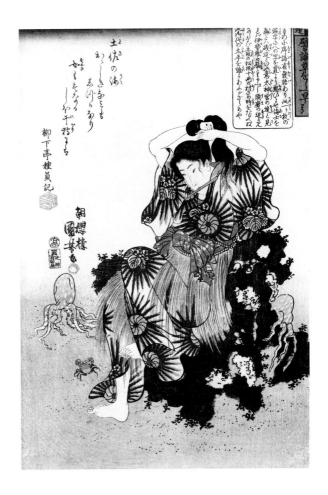

(c. 1843, fig. 24) parallels Yasuo's *Sleeping Beauty* (1924,
fig. 25) with its scene of a solitary bather juxtaposed with
octopi in a horizonless space. The younger Kuniyoshi
heightens the sexual tension of the encounter by having
the octopus slide one tentacle through the water to caress
the nude under her breast, echoing nineteenth-century
Japanese prints that depict erotic encounters between
women and octopi.[51] Even with its two smiling cupids
and its female nude, rendered with volumetric light and
shade—all elements from the European tradition—one
can imagine that this drawing would have looked quite
alien to the audience of Kuniyoshi's 1925 show at the
Daniel Gallery.

FIG. 25
Yasuo Kuniyoshi, *Sleeping Beauty*, 1924, pen and ink, brush and ink, and graphite on paper, 14 x 19¾ in. (35.6 x 50.2 cm),
Collection of Whitney Museum of American Art, New York, gift of Mrs. Edith Gregor Halpert

FIG. 26
Utagawa Kuniyoshi,
*Water Creatures: Octopus
Clutching a Rock*,
1837-42, vertical oban
diptych, 14¾ x 5 in.
(37.1 x 12.4 cm),
Museum of Fine Arts,
Springfield, Massachusetts,
Raymond Bidwell
Collection

FIG. 27
Yasuo Kuniyoshi, *Octopus*, 1922, pen and ink, brush and
ink on paper, 20 x 12 in. (50.8 x 30.5 cm), photograph
courtesy of Sara Kuniyoshi

A similar parallel can be drawn between Utagawa
Kuniyoshi's *Octopus Clutching a Rock* (1837-42, fig. 26)
and Yasuo's *Octopus* (1922, fig. 27). The elder Kuniyoshi
exploited the traditional Japanese vertical format and the
motion of the water to superb decorative effect. The
younger created a submarine narrative in which two fish
at the right watch an octopus menacing a little fish at the
top, as a crayfish at the lower left pinches a tentacle; this
in turn makes the octopus release a cloud of black ink
that threatens the little fish above. Yasuo represented the
octopus' ink by simply spreading ink on the middle of
the page, creating a sophisticated pun on the literal nature
of the medium and its depictive function. This type of
artistic self-consciousness is quite alien to the Japanese
tradition but is an essential part of modernism. Its
presence here makes this drawing one of Kuniyoshi's
most profound fusions of the two cultures.[52]

Lady Slipper (1924, pl. 17) is a beautiful example of
the close-up nature drawings Kuniyoshi also was making
in this period, using ink and occasionally some added
color. Seen from the insect equivalent of Field's "crab's
point of view," these drawings have extensive precedents
in Japanese art, such as Bompo Gyokuen's fifteenth-
century sumi ink drawing, *Orchids and Rock* (fig. 28).[53]
In *Lady Slipper* Kuniyoshi stressed the flower's veined,

yellow, engorged lip and placed it so it towers over a
distant landscape with a tiny bare tree and mountain
peaks that hover in the sky and dissolve into atmosphere
before they reach the ground. Mountains of this type are a
staple of Chinese and Japanese landscape painting, as seen
in an example by Sesshu (fig. 29), an artist from Okayama
whose work Kuniyoshi especially admired.

In 1932 Donald Deskey hired Kuniyoshi to decorate
the walls of the Ladies Powder Room in Radio City Music
Hall. Deskey designed the mirrors and the furniture while
Kuniyoshi painted the murals, as together they created
what is still one of the little-known Art Deco treasures
of New York (fig. 30). Kuniyoshi was given the job after

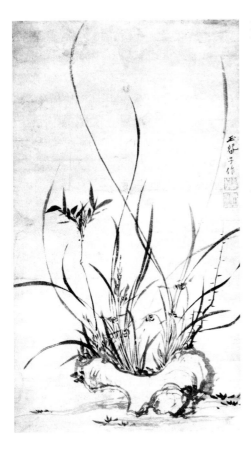

FIG. 28
Bompo Gyokuen,
Orchids and Rock, early
15th century, ink on
paper, 39¼ x 15 in.
(99.8 x 38.2 cm), private
collection, Japan,
photograph courtesy of
Okayama Prefectural
Museum of Art, Okayama,
Japan

FIG. 29
Sesshu, *Landscape in
Haboku Style*, Muromachi
period, dated 1495,
8 x 10 in. (20.3 x 25.4 cm),
Kyoryokukai,
Tokyo National Museum,
Tokyo, Japan

FIG. 30
Yasuo Kuniyoshi, murals for Ladies Powder Room, Radio City Music Hall, completed in 1932,
photograph courtesy of Sara Kuniyoshi

FIG 31
Robert Laurent, *Swamp Lily*, 1922, walnut, 20 in. high
(50.8 cm), Collection of John Laurent, image reproduced
from the exhibition catalogue, *The Robert Laurent Memorial
Exhibition* (1973), with permission from The Art Gallery,
University of New Hampshire

Georgia O'Keeffe had accepted and then withdrawn from
it, leading the few recent writers who have mentioned
this room to suggest that Kuniyoshi's scheme of enlarged
flowers related to O'Keeffe's famous floral images.[54] But
Kuniyoshi's drawings of the early 1920s make it clear that
he drew on his own artistic past to paint this mirage-like
interior with its huge flowers and small mountain peaks
dissolving above them. Painting all the walls and the
ceiling, he created a magical environment that has no
parallel among the hundreds of murals produced by
American artists during the Depression years.

Kuniyoshi's close-up views of foliage had countless
precedents in earlier Japanese art, but they also had
companions within the artist's American cultural circle.
His friend Robert Laurent, who had learned about
Japanese art from Field and inherited his mentor's
collection, carved some remarkable wood sculptures
of leaves in the early 1920s (fig. 31). These can be seen
as three-dimensional counterparts of Kuniyoshi's plant
drawings. When sculptor Alfeo Faggi wrote the catalogue
foreword for Laurent's 1922 exhibition at the Bourgeois
Gallery, he characterized the sculptor's works in terms
that apply to Kuniyoshi's as well:

> In the sculpture of Robert Laurent at last we have
> the break with the Greco-Roman traditions and,
> at the same time, we find that he has brought into
> his art the exquisite feeling, the sensitiveness, the
> metaphysical point of view which characterises the
> art of the Orient. It is the same phenomenon as
> marks the work of the painter "Rousseau le
> douanier."[55]

Faggi rejected the Greco-Roman tradition, the precursor
of Renaissance realism, in favor of something more abstract, as found in Asian art. Comparable in value was
the folk art of Henri Rousseau, beloved by Picasso and
the Parisian modernists. This is the aesthetic context in
which Kuniyoshi and his friends made their art, inspired
by Hamilton Easter Field and his multicultural ideals.

In April 1925, after his fourth show at Daniel's,
Kuniyoshi took his first trip to Europe. After what he
described as the "most uproarious party I have ever been
to," thrown for them by Juliana Force, Kuniyoshi and

Katherine Schmidt sailed to Paris.[56] They would spend
eight months abroad, a period during which Kuniyoshi,
affected by the art he saw, would make decisive changes in
his painting. He began to work directly from the model
instead of from his imagination, inaugurating a new phase
in his career and bringing to an end the brilliant period of
his first artistic maturity, the early 1920s.

Notes

. . . .

Much of the research for this essay was made possible thanks to an Andrew W. Mellon Fellowship
from the Metropolitan Museum of Art in 1992.

1 Yasuo Kuniyoshi, *Yasuo Kuniyoshi* (New York: American Artists Group, 1945), n.p. The same text was published as "East to West," *Magazine of Art* 33 (February 1940).

2 Ibid.

3 Alexander Brook, "Yasuo Kuniyoshi—A Tribute," in *Yasuo Kuniyoshi, 1889-1953* (Austin: The University of Texas at Austin, 1975), p. 51.

4 Lloyd Goodrich, interviews with Yasuo Kuniyoshi, January 6, 1948, in Artist Files, Whitney Museum of American Art, New York.

5 Mrs. Irvine Shubert (Katherine Schmidt), letter to Sara Mazo Kuniyoshi, February 21, 1977, Kuniyoshi Papers, Archives of American Art, Smithsonian Institution (hereafter Kuniyoshi Papers, AAA), not microfilmed.

6 Years later Kuniyoshi wrote of Miller, "I can remember very distinctly his introducing me to Daumier's drawings, and my trying to grasp their full meaning and significance." Kuniyoshi, *Kuniyoshi*, n.p.

7 Lloyd Goodrich cites Louis Bouché, who told him that artists called it the Penguin rather than the Penguin Club. Goodrich, typescript, Goodrich Archives from Whitney Museum of American Art, Archives of American Art, Smithsonian Institution (hereafter Goodrich Archives, AAA), reel N-670, frames 20-21.

8 Kuniyoshi, *Kuniyoshi*, n.p.

9 See Sidney Geist, "The Fireman's Ball for Brancusi," *Archives of American Art Journal* 16, no. 1 (1976): 8-11.

10 William Rubin, "Appendix, The Library of Hamilton Easter Field," *Picasso and Braque, Pioneering Cubism* (New York: The Museum of Modern Art, 1989), pp. 63-69.

11 For a valuable discussion of the American art colony phenomenon, see Karal Ann Marling, "Introduction," *Woodstock, An American Art Colony, 1902-1977* (Poughkeepsie, N.Y.: Vassar College Art Gallery, 1977).

12 For the history of Ogunquit as an art colony, see Louise Tragard, Patricia E. Hart, and W. L. Copithorne, *A Century of Color, 1886-1986* (Ogunquit, Maine: Barn Gallery Associates, Inc., 1987).

13 Robert Laurent, Laurent Papers, Archives of American Art, Smithsonian Institution, reel 2065, frames 267-268.

14 Lloyd Goodrich, notes on an interview with Katherine Schmidt conducted in February 1948, Goodrich Archives, AAA, reel N-670, frames 22-23. This is the source of some material that follows on the early years of the Kuniyoshi marriage.

15 Arnold Blanch, interview by Dorothy Seckler, tape recording, Woodstock, N.Y., June 13, 1963, transcript in Archives of American Art, p. 16.

16 Kuniyoshi, *Kuniyoshi*, n.p.

17 Brook, "Kuniyoshi—A Tribute," p. 54.

18 There is a little ambiguity as to the date of Kuniyoshi's first group exhibition with Daniel. Records of the gallery are sparse, and the catalogue of the exhibition in question reads "Opening Exhibition 1920-21, Closing November 16," so presumably it was in late 1920.

19 Goodrich interview with Kuniyoshi, Whitney Museum.

20 Anonymous, *Sun*, January 7, 1922, in Kuniyoshi Papers, AAA, reel D-176, frame 80. This review also compares Kuniyoshi with Albert Bloch.

21 Hartley was also well aware of the German folk tradition of "hinterglas malerei" that his German acquaintances, Franz Marc and Wassily Kandinsky, admired.

22 Anonymous, *New York Times Book Review and Magazine*, January 15, 1922, in Kuniyoshi Papers, AAA, reel D-176, frame 80.

23 *Sun*, January 7, 1922, Kuniyoshi Papers, AAA, reel D-176, frame 80.

24 Anonymous, "Exhibitions That Forecast an Epidemic of Modernism," *World*, January 15, 1922, in Kuniyoshi Papers, AAA, reel D-187, frame 87.

25 William Murrell, *Yasuo Kuniyoshi*, in Younger Artists Series, Number 4 (Woodstock, N.Y.: William M. Fisher, 1922), n.p.

26 Kuniyoshi, *Kuniyoshi*, n.p.

27 This observation was suggested by Sara Mazo Kuniyoshi, the artist's second wife. For the scarcity of cows in Japan, see Basil Hall Chamberlain, *Things Japanese, Being Notes on Various Subjects Connected with Japan* (London: John Murray, 1905), p. 19, and *Japan at the Beginning of the Twentieth Century*, compiled by the Department of Agriculture and Commerce (London: 1904), p. 184. Thank you to Jane Myers for these references.

28 Henry McBride, "Japanese Exhibits Individual Works," *New York Herald*, January 13, 1924, in Kuniyoshi Papers, AAA, reel D-176, frame 143.

29 Ibid.

30 Anonymous, "Two Brooklynites in Diverse Exhibitions," *Brooklyn Daily Eagle*, January 13, 1924, in Kuniyoshi Papers, AAA, reel D-176, frame 145.

31 Anonymous, in Kuniyoshi Papers, AAA, reel D-176, frame 145; see also, from reel D-176, "Symbolic Drawing by Yasuo Kuniyoshi," *New York Evening Post*, January 12, 1924, frame 144, and "Yasuo Kuniyoshi," *Art News*, 1924, frame 144; the quote is from "Kuniyoshi Has Sense of Humor; Japanese Artist Uses Western Idiom for Eastern Wit," *Sunday World*, [n.d.], frame 144.

32 "Yasuo Kuniyoshi," *New York Times*, 1924, in Kuniyoshi Papers, AAA, reel D-176, frame 144.

33 Jean Paul Slusser, *Bernard Karfiol* (New York: Whitney Museum of American Art, n.d.), p. 7.

34 Daniel Gallery, *Recent Paintings and Drawings by Yasuo Kuniyoshi*, closing January 22, 1924, in Kuniyoshi Papers, AAA, reel D-176, frames 140-141.

35 Ibid.

36 For a good discussion of the relation between Kuniyoshi's paintings and American folk art, see Susan Lubowsky, "From Naiveté to Maturity: 1906-1939," *Yasuo Kuniyoshi* (Kyoto: The National Museum of Modern Art, 1989), pp. 23-24.

37 Tom Armstrong, "The Innocent Eye: American Folk Sculpture," in *Two Hundred Years of American Sculpture* (New York: Whitney Museum of American Art, 1976), p. 85, and Avis Berman, *Rebels on Eighth Street, Juliana Force and The Whitney Museum of American Art* (New York: Atheneum, 1990), p. 201. Berman's book is the source of much of the information in this paragraph.

38 Whitney Studio Club, *Catalogue of an Exhibition of Early American Art*, in Kuniyoshi papers, AAA, reel D-176, frames 148-151.

39 The catalogue microfilmed in the Kuniyoshi Papers, AAA (reel D-176, frames 155-156) is incomplete; the final page is missing. The original can be found in Kuniyoshi's scrapbook, collection of Sara Kuniyoshi. The reviews are mostly anonymous, found in the Kuniyoshi Papers, AAA, reel D-176, frames 172, 250, 263.

40 Henry McBride, "Robust Art of Yasuo Kuniyoshi," January 3, 1925, in Kuniyoshi Papers, AAA, reel D-176, frame 167.

41 Kuniyoshi, *Kuniyoshi*, n.p.

42 "The Third Dimension in Painting: A Lecture by Kenneth Hayes Miller," in Lincoln Rothschild, *To Keep Art Alive: The Effort of Kenneth Hayes Miller* (Philadelphia: The Art Alliance Press, 1974), p. 80. However, Miller did recommend a book of reproductions of Chinese art to Isabel Bishop as a standard for color; Sheldon Reich, *Isabel Bishop* (Tucson: University of Arizona Museum of Art, 1974), p. 31.

43 For Field, see Doreen Bolger, "Hamilton Easter Field and His Contribution to American Modernism," *American Art Journal* 20, no. 2 (1988): 79-107. Bolger's research papers, given by her to the Portland Museum of Art, Portland, Maine, and her Master's thesis, "Hamilton Easter Field and the Rise of Modern Art in America" (University of Delaware, 1973), have been very helpful to this essay.

44 Hamilton Easter Field, *The Technique of Oil Painting and Other Essays* (Brooklyn, New York: Ardsley House, 1918), pp. 79ff.

45 Hamilton Easter Field, "Comment on the Arts" (reviewing December 1921), *Arts* 2, no. 3 (1922): 172.

46 Hamilton Easter Field, "The Pennsylvania Academy," *Arts* 1 (February-March 1921): 24.

47 Henry McBride described the shroud in *Self-Portrait* as "an unusual instance of atavism. . . . The hooded Japanese head is remarkably true in style to the masterly hooded heads that appear so frequently in early Japanese prints and painting." "Robust Art of Yasuo Kuniyoshi," unidentified clipping, Kuniyoshi Papers, AAA, reel D-176, frame 167.

48 I am grateful to Katsumi Seeno, Curator at the Okayama Prefectural Museum, for pointing this out to me.

49 When listing his preferences among artists, Kuniyoshi made up an international list: "Seshu [*sic*], Korin, Chinese sculptures, Courbet, Signorelli, Daumier and Delacroix." Samuel Kootz, *Modern American Painters* (New York: Brewer and Warren, Inc., 1930), p. 43. Ogata Korin's *Shinrai* is accompanied by a second panel depicting Tatsumi Kaze, the Wind God, also in the Tokyo National Museum.

50 Hamilton Easter Field, "The Art of Kuniyoshi," *Arts and Decoration* 7 (March 1917): 251.

51 Theodore Bowie, "Erotic Aspects of Japanese Art," *Studies in Erotic Art* (New York: Basic Books Inc., 1971), pp. 191ff., fig. 107. Thanks to Lowery Sims, Curator at the Metropolitan Museum of Art, for bringing this reference to my attention.

52 The location of this drawing is currently unknown. Kuniyoshi's association of the octopus with Japan is underlined by a series of propaganda drawings he made during World War II for the Office of War Information. Titled *Clean Up This Mess*, they feature a huge hand holding a bag of garbage whose contents represent Japanese militarism: samurai swords, Japanese flags, and octopi.

53 This is a complex issue. Close-up views of tiny areas of landscape can be found in Western art (for example, in Albrecht Dürer's watercolors and in the detailed nature paintings of the nineteenth-century American Pre-Raphaelites), but here they seem like occasional novelties as opposed to a centuries-old way to view the world. In addition, when this insect's eye scrutiny of a patch of nature appears in Western art, it is usually rendered with microscopic realist detail, as opposed to the more general-ized and decorative approach common in Japanese art.

54 Benita Eisler, *O'Keeffe and Stieglitz: An American Romance* (New York: Doubleday, 1991), p. 346; Laurie Lisle, *Portrait of an Artist: A Biography of Georgia O'Keeffe* (New York: Washington Square Press, 1981), p. 261.

55 Alfeo Faggi, "Foreword," *Exhibition of Sculptures by Robert Laurent* (New York: Bourgeois Galleries, 1922).

56 Lloyd Goodrich, *Yasuo Kuniyoshi* (New York: Whitney Museum of American Art, 1948), p. 25.

PLATE **21**

Eggplant, 1921, pen and ink, brush and ink on paper,
14⅝ x 10⁹⁄₁₆ in. (37.2 x 26.5 cm), The University of Iowa
Museum of Art, Iowa City, Museum Purchase

PLATE 22

Baby and Toy Cow, 1921, pen and ink, brush and ink on paper,
12⅛ x 9⅜ in. (30.8 x 23.8 cm), The Brooklyn Museum,
bequest of Edith and Milton Lowenthal

PLATE 23

Three Cows and One Calf, 1922, pen and ink, brush and ink,
and graphite on paper, 15½ x 22½ in. (39.4 x 57.1 cm),
Smith College Museum of Art, Northampton, Massachusetts,
gift of Philip L. Goodwin, 1953

PLATE 24

The Calf Doesn't Want to Go, 1922, pen and ink, brush and ink
on paper, 15⅜ x 22⅝ in. (39.1 x 57.5 cm), The Museum of
Modern Art, New York, The Katherine S. Dreier Bequest

PLATE 25

Boy with Cow, 1922, pen and ink, brush and ink on paper,
14⅝ x 20⅞ in. (37.2 x 51.8 cm), Collection of
Robert Hull Fleming Museum, University of Vermont,
Burlington, gift of Henry Schnakenberg

PLATE 26

Remains of Lunch, 1922, pen and ink, brush and ink
on paper, 12½ x 9¼ in. (31.8 x 23.5 cm),
Mary Lublin Fine Arts and Franklin Riehlman, New York

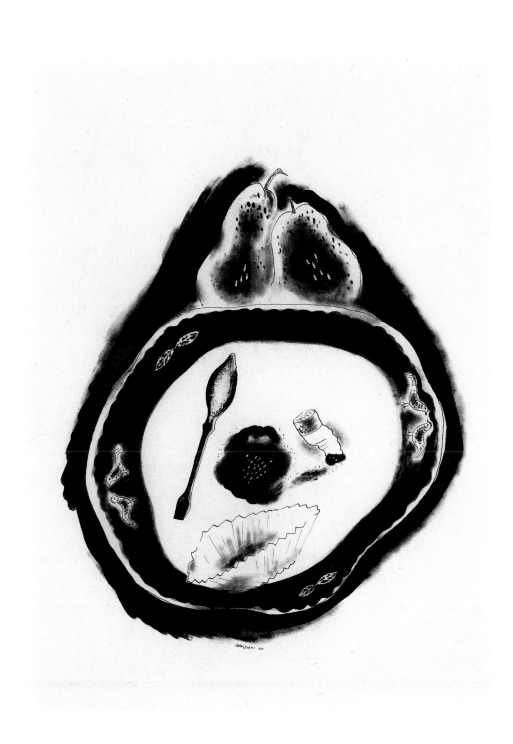

PLATE 27

Bedroom, 1922, pen and ink, brush and ink, and
charcoal on paper, 19¾ x 15¼ in. (50.2 x 38.7 cm),
The Saint Louis Art Museum

PLATE 28

Morning Glory and Weeds, 1922, pen and ink, brush and ink on paper, 15¼ x 11¼ in. (38.7 x 28.6 cm), Whitney Museum of American Art, New York, Felicia Meyer Marsh Bequest

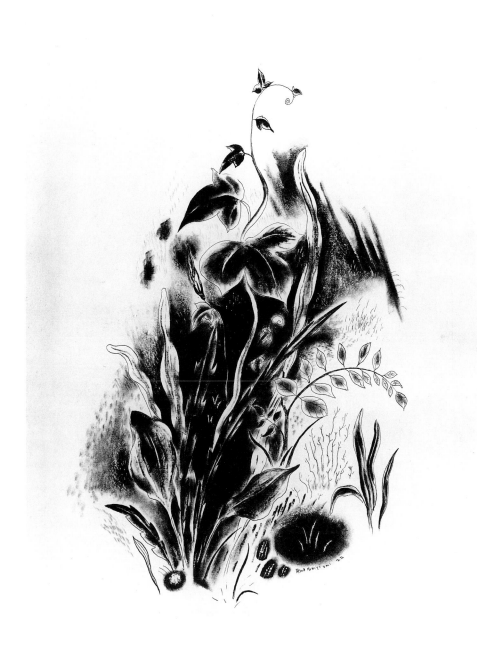

PLATE 29

The Dream, 1922, pen and ink, brush and ink, and graphite on
paper, 22⅜ x 15⅜ in. (56.8 x 39.1 cm), Amon Carter Museum,
Fort Worth, Texas

PLATE 30

Bad Dream, 1924, pen and ink, brush and ink, and
graphite on paper, 24 x 30 in. (61 x 76.2 cm), The Ogunquit
Museum of American Art, Ogunquit, Maine

P<small>LATE</small> **31**

Fisherman, 1924, pen and ink, brush and ink on paper,
22 x 28⅜ in. (55.8 x 72 cm), The Museum of Modern Art,
New York, given anonymously (by exchange)

Plant, 1925, pen and ink, brush and ink, and graphite
on paper, 22¼ x 15¼ in. (56.5 x 38.7 cm), The Museum of
Modern Art, New York, gift of Abby Aldrich Rockefeller

54

PLATE 33

Artichoke, 1925, pen and ink, brush and ink, and graphite
on paper, 15¼ x 22³⁄₁₆ in. (38.7 x 56.4 cm), Elvehjem Museum
of Art, University of Wisconsin-Madison

Independent Creations:
Kuniyoshi's Ink Drawings of 1921-25

Jane Myers

At the outset of his artistic career, Yasuo Kuniyoshi developed a distinctive pen, brush, and ink style that he used in over sixty highly finished exhibition drawings. Dating between 1921 and 1925, these remarkably sophisticated works are early representations of an aesthetic conviction the artist expressed later in his life, that drawing "is an independent creation, an intimate expression. . . It requires infinitely more knowledge to produce a drawing, which in itself speaks as eloquently as a painting, without relying on color."[1]

Perhaps unique among the American modernists who were his contemporaries, Kuniyoshi regarded his pen and ink drawings as complete, individual statements. Even though they sometimes shared imagery with his oil paintings, they were unlike the more cursory graphite sketches in which he recorded preliminary ideas for these larger works (see fig. 12 and pl. 1).[2] The fact that he later could not recall whether he executed the ink drawing *The Dream* (1922, pl. 29) before or after the oil titled *Dream* (1922, pl. 2) further indicates that the drawing, while sharing common imagery with the painting, did not serve a preparatory function for the oil.[3]

Today virtually unknown, Kuniyoshi's ink drawings attracted accolades when he first exhibited them, for both his evident mastery of technique and his idiosyncratic subject matter. To the viewer of the 1920s, these works posed a perplexing conundrum that still persists today. At first glance, the drawings appear accessible, even facile, yet closer examination reveals a more complicated and elusive quality. In his peculiar choices of subject and their treatment, he evinces an understated humor and a highly personal vision, seemingly touched by another culture outside the experience of minds steeped in Western civilization.

The ink drawings Kuniyoshi produced in the brief period between 1921, when he created works for his first one-man exhibition at the Daniel Gallery, and 1925, the year he departed for his first trip to France, form a discrete group. In France, where he remained for nine months, Kuniyoshi turned from drawing the fantastic imagery that distinguishes much of his early work to

FIG. 32
Yasuo Kuniyoshi, *Girl on Sofa*, 1925, oil on canvas, 36¾ x 43 in. (93.4 x 109.2 cm), University Art Collections, Arizona State University, Oliver B. James, 1951

painting naturalistic subjects, predominantly the female figure (fig. 32). In the decades that followed, drawings were less prominent in Kuniyoshi's total output, until, after World War II, he again became interested in the ink medium.[4]

Kuniyoshi took up drawing within a favorable artistic climate for the various drawing media—watercolor the most prominent among them. During the first two decades of the century, the impresario of modernism, Alfred Stieglitz, had laid the groundwork for drawing's heightened esteem. Through his gallery 291, from 1905 to 1917, Stieglitz cultivated a sympathetic environment for works on paper. He showed the work of modern European artists, including Matisse, Cézanne, and Rodin, and pastels, watercolors, and black and white drawings by Americans working in avant-garde styles—Arthur Dove, John Marin, Abraham Walkowitz, and Georgia O'Keeffe among them. Works on paper continued to rise, albeit gradually and on a limited scale, in both critical and popular estimation. One art critic defensively observed: "Drawings. Yes, just drawings. There is steadily growing

FIG. 33
Joseph Stella, *Peonies*, c. 1919, silverpoint and crayon,
23⅛ x 18½ in. (58.7 x 47 cm), Amon Carter Museum,
Fort Worth, Texas, gift of Ruth Carter Stevenson

an appreciation for drawings and other so-called slight
works of art by important artists." He noted the medium's
improving stature while inadvertently reinforcing its
traditional position as preliminary study: "A drawing
usually has more imagination than the finished work."[5]

American artists chose works on paper for some of
their most innovative, independent expressions. During
the early to mid-1920s, the expanding circle of artists
who made their creative mark through a rich array of
drawing media included Edward Hopper and Charles
Burchfield, both of whom featured watercolors in their
successful New York exhibitions. Regular exhibitions
of the Whitney Studio Club, formed in 1918, also
highlighted works on paper; the drawings of artists like
Peggy Bacon and Joseph Stella (fig. 33), although widely
divergent stylistically, paralleled the work of Kuniyoshi
in the precision of their draftsmanship.

Kuniyoshi's ink drawings made an important
contribution to this creative environment. Like other
progressive artists of his day, he expanded the boundaries
of an under-regarded medium, creating a rich array of
textures and tonalities in essentially monochromatic ink.
Pen and brush were his expressive tools for exaggerated
forms and whimsical juxtapositions. Kuniyoshi infused
even inanimate subjects with an unmistakable, often
otherworldly, vitality, transcending otherwise mundane
still lifes and narratives through his imaginative compositions and extraordinary technical ability.

Like the best drawings of the period, including the
work of Charles Sheeler, Charles Demuth, and O'Keeffe,
Kuniyoshi's works on paper expressed a highly personal
edge—in his case, the evocation of distant memory. Although his "exotic" modernism is more conservative than
that of the traditionally accepted avant-garde artists, his
drawings and theirs revealed both the artist's personality
and his understanding of his subject's inner essence. This
quality was intrinsic to modernism as it had evolved in
America the previous decade.

As with the modernists whose merits Stieglitz
propounded, Kuniyoshi was fortunate to find his niche
despite the rather limited opportunities to showcase
contemporary art. Soon after he completed his studies at
the Art Students League in New York, he attracted the

attention of Charles Daniel, one of the more important
dealers to support the work of young artists. Featuring
Kuniyoshi's work in annual exhibitions beginning in early
1922, Daniel was one of the many critics who applauded
his "superb" drawings.[6] Kuniyoshi's active participation in
the artistic circle of Hamilton Easter Field, his patron
until Field's untimely death in 1922, also encouraged the
young artist's innovative approach by exposing him to the
art and theory of contemporary movements.[7]

The positive reception for Kuniyoshi's drawings, as
well as their creation, was conditioned not only by the
growing acceptance of the drawing medium and the
emphasis on original expression, but by a fascination with
Japan, where Kuniyoshi was born in 1889 and lived until
1906. During the late teens and early twenties, East Coast
cultural circles embraced a profusion of art exhibitions,
plays, novels, poetry, and dance performances dealing
with Japanese culture. Produced by both Japanese and
Americans, these events sparked American interest in
Japan, which had not waned since Commodore Matthew
Perry's arrival there in 1854.

Beginning in the late nineteenth century, prominent
American scholars and teachers like Ernest Fenellosa and
Arthur Wesley Dow developed a fondness for Japanese art
and aesthetics, which soon became a powerful influence
in American art curricula and museum collections.
Japanese simplicity of form was a valued component of
the modernist approach that Dow imparted to his
students, including O'Keeffe. Japan represented a higher

level of artistic discernment; its poetic language, for
example, was considered "utterly distinct from the sick
languors of the eighteen-nineties. It is crisp and terse, rich
and brief."[8] However, Kuniyoshi was in the nearly unique
position of developing his affinity for Japanese models
through direct experience, both as a youth in Japan
and through continuing contact with Asian culture in
America. The Japanese attributes of Kuniyoshi's work
were especially evident in his drawings, which appropri-
ated general, though not specific, forms of Asian art.
Thus, Kuniyoshi's drawing of an orange (1925, pl. 20),
O'Keeffe's *Green Apple on Black Plate* (c. 1921, fig. 34),
and an Asian antecedent (fig. 35) reveal a compatible
artistic point of view.

The perception of Eastern aesthetics was highly
romanticized during Kuniyoshi's early years in America,[9]
and critics tended to see exotic cultural characteristics in
his early work. One noted: "In Yasuo Kuniyoshi's initial
one-man show at Daniel's, the Orient and the Occident
meet and embrace like long lost brothers."[10] Kuniyoshi's
emerging career as an artist coincided with the rise of
American cultural nationalism following World War I,
as artists and intellectuals searched for the qualities that
reflected their authentic Americanness. In an echo of
nativist sentiment, critics praised Kuniyoshi for ultimately
neglecting European forms of Post-Impressionism and
remaining true to his Japanese roots.[11]

The incentive for Kuniyoshi to allude to Japanese
precedents was, therefore, not insignificant. The ink
medium provided the means to combine personal subjects
with his "exotic" heritage in a way that resonated with
critics and the public. In overall appearance and form, if
not his specific technique, Kuniyoshi's application of the
ink medium invokes traditional sumi ink drawing, known
as *sumi-e*, for which the sumi stick, a compressed cake of
black soot, is rubbed with water to produce a rich black
ink. *Sumi-e* is a centuries-old Chinese and Japanese form
of drawing, noteworthy for its simplicity of expression,
highly controlled brushstrokes, and tonal gradations
achieved through a fluid application of ink (fig. 35).
In choosing a black-and-white method, Kuniyoshi
conformed to his contemporaries' perception that "the
Oriental mind accepts monochrome as the highest form

of art."[12] In later years, he acknowledged that he may have been inspired to render finished black and white drawings because of his strong Asian antecedents.[13]

Yet the manner in which Kuniyoshi applied ink with brush and pen was distinctively his own and only superficially related to the Asian technique. His richly textured surfaces and emphasis on detail (especially in his earliest drawings) diverge from traditional Japanese artists' more direct, pure application of the ink medium. Kuniyoshi approached ink drawing as if it were watercolor, employing subtractive methods of scraping and blotting to create various textures. He chose Whatman paper of moderate weight—a durable, high-quality sheet that was receptive to his manipulations.[14]

In selecting a technique associated with watercolor applications, Kuniyoshi may have been expressing an admiration for Winslow Homer, whose work Hamilton Easter Field collected. Field considered Homer an exemplar of "sincerity" in American art for his blending of skillful technique with an honest lifestyle.[15] Homer's desire to live among fishermen and to paint the life he knew appealed to Field, who insisted that his own coterie of artists—including Kuniyoshi and his wife, the painter Katherine Schmidt—reside among the fishermen at their summer artists' colony in Ogunquit, Maine. In addition to the Homer watercolors in Field's collection, Kuniyoshi could have seen the great nineteenth-century artist's watercolors while wintering in Brooklyn Heights, New York. The nearby Brooklyn Museum included Homer's works in its 1921 exhibition devoted to the modern watercolor.[16]

The compatibility of modernism and a Japanese aesthetic is conspicuous in one of Kuniyoshi's earliest drawings, *Baby and Toy Cow* (1921, pl. 22), which presents several thematic preoccupations from the artist's Ogunquit summers. The entire arrangement echoes the shape of the most overt Japanese reference in the image, the circular yin-yang symbol. Around it rotate the three major elements of the composition: a toy cow, a sailboat, and an apparently Asian child crawling on a blanket that depicts a barren tree and waves lapping against a shoreline. Echoing the yin-yang design are the child's undulating hairline and the overall composition, which

balances the highly developed area at the lower right with the blankness of the rest of the white sheet. This asymmetrical composition appeals to both Japanese and American modernist sensibilities. Furthermore, the child and cow would become signature motifs for the artist, conveying tantalizingly autobiographical suggestions.

Covert autobiographical references abound in Kuniyoshi's ink drawings. *Bedroom* (pl. 27), one of over twenty ink drawings he executed in 1922, was probably exhibited late that year as *The Black Curtain* in the "Exhibition of Paintings, Watercolors, Drawings, and Etchings of Interiors" at the Belmaison Gallery of Decorative Arts, in Wanamaker's New York department store. Kuniyoshi's friend and fellow artist Louis Bouché, who served as director of the gallery, was given "carte blanche" to feature work by vanguard artists. The gallery was not planned to turn a profit but rather to enhance Wanamaker's support of the arts.[17]

Kuniyoshi lavished great care on *Bedroom*, whose subject, atypical for the artist, was likely a response to Bouché's designated theme of the interior. The drawing contains both minute pen and ink details and a commanding, broadly brushed curtain. Among its meticulously detailed components are the fringed cloth draped over a small table, delicate striations of the table's wood-grained surfaces, decorative designs on the water pitcher and on the chamber pot beneath the rumpled bed, and a carpet bearing both a fish and calligraphic marks echoing Japanese textile design. Through the open window, a tiny fence, plant, barren tree, and sharply rectilinear buildings jostle for position, while fine incised lines create tiny window panes that further define the foreground building.[18] These myriad fine details contrast sharply with the densely inked curtain swags that dominate the modest room, their independent, voluminous, wavelike folds suggesting the burgeoning organic forms of O'Keeffe's contemporary work. To accentuate the curtains, Kuniyoshi built up pools of ink in areas he wished to intensify; this effect is even more marked because the binder has risen to the ink's surface and created glossy passages that gently give way to edges feathered with a dry brush.[19]

As in *Baby and Toy Cow* (pl. 22), quixotic details beg a symbolic reading of the ostensibly commonplace. The drawing's elevated view through the window suggests a multi-story dwelling as the setting—possibly the Brooklyn Heights brownstone owned by Hamilton Easter Field, where Kuniyoshi and Katherine Schmidt lived adjacent to their patron. The geometrically defined buildings that appear through the window also suggest Ogunquit, whose vernacular structures Kuniyoshi often simplified into rectilinear building blocks (as in *Maine Family*, pl. 4, and *Cows in Pasture*, pl. 6). The drawing's sharply tilted perspective and the jumble of stacked buildings relate to Kuniyoshi's favored compositions in his landscape oils of that year, such as *Upstream* (pl. 3), and were specific motifs favored by American artists experimenting with Cubism.[20] The spectral, densely inked curtain swags in this 1922 drawing may allude to Field's unexpected death in the spring of that year—an interpretation somewhat reinforced by the drawing's original title, *The Black Curtain*. Kuniyoshi's association with Field was close; the older man was the first to support him financially, thus enabling him to devote himself to his artistic career and quit the odd jobs he had been doing to generate income.

For the most part, Kuniyoshi would leave somber metaphors for his later career, in works that addressed his response to World War II. Far more commonly, his early drawings had a humorous dimension. *Remains of Lunch* (1922, pl. 26) unpretentiously depicts the aftermath of a light repast: a luncheon plate bears a fluted paper pastry cup, a demitasse spoon, a dollop of fruit sauce, and a retired cigarette butt.[21] The placement of two pears above the plate, which is decorated with pairs of leaves and birds, suggests that the pair/pear double entendre is intentional. The dish also recalls rising interest in folk arts and crafts, which Field, Kuniyoshi, and others in their circle actively collected.

The humorous, ironic tone of such drawings suggests several cultural and artistic contexts. Between 1915 and 1922 the Dadaists—Marcel Duchamp and Man Ray preeminent among them—brought their nihilistic, ambiguous humor to New York art circles. Where the Dadaists were notorious for their provocative and defiant artistic jokes, however, Kuniyoshi used whimsy and

trickery. He would later deny the humorous content seemingly intertwined with this playful approach, yet in the early 1920s his friends, including Alexander Brook and Louis Bouché, drew notice as a new generation of artists who, in choosing subject matter, "have decided that art is not necessarily a deadly serious thing." As Brook recalled the period: "It was just as interesting to have fun as it was to paint in those days." The fun continued at Ogunquit. From Maine, Betty Burroughs wrote to Reginald Marsh—whom she would later marry—of their friends, calling Kuniyoshi by his nickname: "Katherine . . . and Yas are very well—in spite of their violent social activities. Life for them is one party after another."[22]

The practice of drawing was intimately tied to high spirits. The male artists who gathered informally as the Penguin, spearheaded by Walt Kuhn, shared with Kuniyoshi a lively camaraderie and a tongue-in-cheek approach: "When the light failed on winter afternoons the Daniel Gallery painters—and it was a very fine stable indeed, consisting of people like Kuniyoshi, Sheeler, Spencer, Demuth, and Preston Dickinson, among others—would gather in the back room, smoke, and talk and laugh. There was a good feeling about."[23] Bawdy spirits dominated the Penguin's weekly evening sketch classes with a live model, and a healthy sense of humor was a prerequisite: "To be a Penguin in good standing, you did not have to be an important artist, but you had to be a good fellow."[24] This group included a number of cartoonists and draftsmen, such as the Bulgarian-born Jules Pascin (1885-1930), a friend of Kuniyoshi's who "enjoyed life around him. . . . Drawing to him was like breathing, he never stopped."[25]

Despite the obvious influence of the young artists in his circle, many observers considered Kuniyoshi's wit to be that of a Japanese humorist taking an amused, even satirical, look at the American lifestyle.[26] No subject was more fraught with comic potential for Kuniyoshi than his early, obsessive predilection for the cow—a distinctly American subject. He had opportunities to scrutinize the beast during summers in Ogunquit, where cows roamed the gently rolling countryside and where the summer winds "brought whiffs of cow pasture and sweet farm smells" from the local dairy farm.[27] Cows appeared in over a dozen of Kuniyoshi's ink drawings between 1921 and 1924, and in numerous early paintings as well. Even in his later career, he believed the cow series to be among his most representative efforts, citing *Cows in Pasture* (pl. 6) for its relationship to his work of the late 1940s and commending its composition and dark palette.[28]

His cow imagery is intriguing in light of an apparently autobiographical association, which Kuniyoshi himself fostered by often mentioning that he was born in the year of the cow. Despite the drawn evidence to the contrary, he later asserted that he did not regard the cow as a source of humor: "I wasn't trying to be funny but everyone thought I was. I was painting cows and cows at that time because somehow I felt very near to the cow."[29] Kuniyoshi often let the animal serve as a narrative device, and sometimes, as in the 1922 drawing *Three Cows and One Calf* (pl. 23), as the sole subject. In this drawing, one of the cows provides nourishment to her calf; perhaps it was the animal Kuniyoshi described (in somewhat flawed English) to Reginald Marsh in a letter expressing his desire to observe cows closely that summer: "Things round here very quiet at present and. . . just [suits]. . . us[.] [W]e started working . . . last week and as usually I begain with cow[.] [S]he presented with a beatiful calf this year which sometimes for me [takes awhile] to get [the] real thing out of them . . . I have made one drawing already and I hope to [find] a way to get [the] real thing out of them some time and probably it means [I will] end this summer with cow."[30]

In *Boy with Cow* (1922, pl. 25), a deceptively simple subject and composition give way, upon close scrutiny, to an unexpected subtlety. The whimsical perspective distorts spatial reality so that an enlarged tropical house-plant towers above the boy. Every detail furthers the understated narrative, which is crowded into one tightly filled space in a larger expanse of blank white paper. *Boy with Cow* reveals Kuniyoshi's sure control of his medium in the sensitive modeling of the boy's face and in the mottled pattern, created through a blotting technique, around the plant forms and on the rocky ground. Kuniyoshi delighted in the variety of shapes and patterns he could achieve: the razor-like precision of the cow's back gives way to miniature

splotches at the tip of its nose, and the decorative, fan-shaped plant resembling wild carrot (*Daucus carota*, also known as Queen Anne's lace) and the spiky cow's tail contrast with the abstract, jagged rocks.[31]

Boy with Cow depicts a psychological drama in which the seemingly wary boy gazes at his bovine companion, insisting that the cow proceed down the rocky incline yet giving the animal the benefit of a slack rope. The docile cow seems endowed with intelligence and a psychological presence. The drawing was likely one of those images exhibited in Kuniyoshi's 1923 exhibition at Daniel Gallery, which also included *The Calf Doesn't Want to Go* (1922, pl. 24). Considered together, the two drawings illustrate a yin-yang relationship of a good versus a bad cow. The protagonist of *The Calf Doesn't Want to Go* is a playful yet stubborn animal with a baby face, emphasized through curvilinear jowls, and diminutive dainty hooves. To accentuate the animal's obstinacy, Kuniyoshi depicts its sharply angular buttocks as it braces against the farmer's firm tug. The vertical striations of the barbed wire motif on the farmer's shirt, amusingly suited to his rural vocation, create an agitated linear pattern that plays off the delicate lines incised into the figure's overalls. The wild carrot plant, with its calligraphic, cupped shape, mimics the rhythmic movement of the farmer swaying to the left as he strains against his adversary. Once again Winslow Homer may have served as an example: his painting *Weaning the Calf* (1875, North Carolina Museum of Art) and related works also depict a boy struggling against an unwilling calf.[32]

Cows are only one narrative element in some of Kuniyoshi's more complex drawings. The fantasy landscapes *The Dream* (1922, pl. 29) and *Bad Dream* (1924, pl. 30) offer dichotomous views of good and evil. In the former, representing the positive forces of the universe, a small girl, arms outstretched, glides heavenward. She casts off from a fanciful landscape overseen by a docile cow, which peacefully cohabits with two snakes—one, tongue darting, nearly camouflaged by the tree trunk around which it is coiled, and a smaller one, again more decorative than menacing, that graces the trunk's roots.

Utilizing a different format and an ostensibly more ominous tone, *Bad Dream* is a fascinating exception

FIG. 36
Yasuo Kuniyoshi, *Leaves*, 1922, pen and ink, brush and ink
on paper, 14½ x 10⅝ in. (37 x 27 cm), Philadelphia Museum
of Art, given by Mrs. Edith Gregor Halpert

among Kuniyoshi's drawings of the early 1920s for its
overt nod to Japanese myth, here combined with a
recapitulation of favored motifs. The innocuous (though
oversized) broad-leaf plants of the earlier drawings are
now transported to a hellish place. One of these plants
shields a demon-like figure near the center of the composition, while similar shapes have metamorphosed into the
wings of the mischievous creatures. The cow assumes
macabre forms; in the lower right portion of the composition, one merges with the body of a creature resembling
a unicorn, while in the upper left, an airborne, one-eyed
cow transports in its mouth a female nude, whose right
foot has been severed. A fish with wings soars through
the upper part of the composition, and snakes, one two-
headed, grow out of incongruent sources—the nearly
barren tree and one of the captives' heads. A few varied
leaves adorn the tree, whose lone fruit recalls the fruit
Eve holds in *Adam and Eve (The Fall of Man)* (pl. 1), another
parable of good and evil. The drawing's botanical pas-
tiches have precedents in Japanese gardening practices, where
dissimilar plants are sometimes grafted onto each other.[33]

The imaginary themes of *The Dream* and *Bad
Dream*, while prevalent in Japanese legend and a wide
range of folk literature, also reflect the modernists'
emphasis on intuition as a creative source and a general
fascination with dreams at a time when Freudian dream
analysis had entered the popular mainstream. In fact,
some commentators, perplexed at the source of the cow
imagery, held Freudian psychology accountable: "Mr.
Kuniyoshi has a complex for cows."[34] Dream imagery by

Odilon Redon, whose work Field collected, and Field's
emphasis on the importance of intuition, particularly in
primitive and children's art, also gave Kuniyoshi ample
impetus to undertake dream sequences.[35] The ease with
which figures fly in the two dream drawings and the
painting (pl. 2) not only suggest a dreamlike state but also
have more specific autobiographical intimations. Among
Kuniyoshi's early experiences in America was learning to
fly while living in Los Angeles. "But everybody I knew
got killed. So I stopped."[36]

The worlds of fantasy and reality merge less con-
spicuously in the detailed outdoor habitats Kuniyoshi
executed in more than a half-dozen close-up, predominantly vertical nature studies (*Morning Glory and Weeds*
[1922, pl. 28]; *Leaves* [1922, fig. 36]; and *Growing Weeds*
[1923, fig. 37]). Because Kuniyoshi and his wife generally

FIG. 37
Yasuo Kuniyoshi, *Growing Weeds*, 1923, pen and ink, brush
and ink, chalk, and watercolor on paper, 13½ x 10½ in.
(34.3 x 26.7 cm), Colby College Museum of Art, Waterville,
Maine, gift of the Edith Gregor Halpert Foundation

remained in Ogunquit into the fall so they could savor
the peaceful atmosphere after the summer crowds departed, the artist was able to witness growth cycles for
a number of indigenous plants. He was especially drawn
to the low vegetation that covered the rocky hillside rising
from the Ogunquit shoreline. In his drawings, Kuniyoshi
tended to combine disparate elements of his environment,
creating arrangements of tropical houseplants and native
flora that did not coexist in the natural environment.

In the drawing *Morning Glory and Weeds* (1922,
pl. 28), the viny tendrils of the morning glory, which
often grows wild in New England, form the central
component of the composition but merge in a single
organic expression with two other plants in the foreground: the snaking shapes of a broad-leafed plant from
the Araceae family and the shorter, broader leaf of the
weedy Plantago family, both of which Kuniyoshi favored
in his images of the period. He used scraping to define
foreground details; his selective and precise blotting
technique for highlighting the tall, narrow leaf forms
echoes the method Demuth employed in his floral watercolors (fig. 38), which were exhibited at the Daniel
Gallery beginning in 1915.[37] Like Demuth, Kuniyoshi
clustered plant elements together to form an organic
whole. Kuniyoshi, however, favored fanciful assemblages
of wild and greenhouse plants, emphasizing decorative
detail and contrasts of light and shade to invoke the
personality of the subjects as he saw them, rather than
enhancing the plant's inherent beauty through an emphasis on color and lush volume.

Kuniyoshi's preference for fancy rather than accuracy
is apparent in such compositions as *Fisherman* (1924,
pl. 31), which provides an even less naturalistic context
for the readily identifiable botanic forms. A fisherman
preparing to gut his catch is surrounded by representatives
of the animal kingdom, including the aquatic realm
where an octopus and fish reside, and by a sampler of
botanical specimens, both wild and cultivated, arrayed
across the sheet. Among the recognizable plants are fern,
horsetail, and orchid, while small-scaled decorative trees,
suggesting the flowering cherry, are executed in a loose,
pointillist style found in traditional Japanese drawing.
Through fantasy Kuniyoshi could allude to both Japanese

and American cultures. The fisherman was a common
figure in Ogunquit, where artists like Kuniyoshi lived
side by side with the hardy seafarers who depended on
the Atlantic for their livelihood. Fishing was also a major industry along the coast of Japan's Inland Sea, the
location of Kuniyoshi's hometown, Okayama, and fish
was a Japanese dietary staple in the late nineteenth
century, as it is today.

An homage to Japan is apparent in the vertical
format of many of Kuniyoshi's botanical works; their
organic existence in an undefined space relates them to
Japanese drawing (see fig. 28). Cultural preferences and
experiences may also have informed his choice of subject.
Just as the rarity of cows in Japan may have led to his
fascination with them in Ogunquit, so wildflowers were
a prototypical American subject. Certainly Kuniyoshi's
immersion in native flora reflects the deep reverence for
nature in Japan, where the art of flower arranging, for
example, conveys philosophic meaning. However,
although certain species, such as the chrysanthemum
and the cherry blossom, have symbolic connotations,
during Kuniyoshi's youth the Japanese did not endow
native wildflowers with a comparable status.[38]

Kuniyoshi's works from 1924-25 tended toward
simplification, emphasizing the more eccentric details of

FIG. 39
Charles Demuth, *Eggplant and Peppers*, 1922, watercolor on
paper, 9¾ x 13¾ in. (24.8 x 34.9 cm), Fisk University Art
Galleries, Nashville, Tennessee, The Alfred Stieglitz Collection
of Modern Art

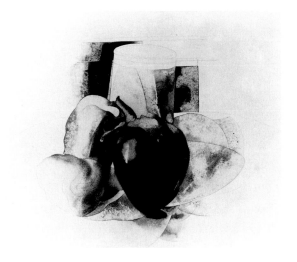

natural forms, as in *Lady Slipper* (1924, pl. 17). Beginning in 1922 or 1923, Kuniyoshi sometimes highlighted
certain features by adding delicate color washes to selected
areas of his rich ink drawings.[39] In *Lady Slipper*, he
emphasizes the flower's pouchlike lip through the
addition of a delicate yellow tint, carefully delineating
its dark veins and adding a light reddish-brown tone
where the lip meets the stem. That Kuniyoshi was
interested in botanical variety but not slavish to scientific
accuracy is evidenced in this work, for the species of
lady's slipper he depicted, *Cypripedium acaule*, is pink,
while the yellow *Cypripedium calceolus* is characterized
by spirally twisted petals.

The prominent organic qualities of *Lady Slipper* are
typical of Kuniyoshi's still lifes of 1924-25, which often
include sexual allusions. *Dish with Banana* (pl. 16) depicts
a piece of deteriorating fruit lying slack in a footed dish.
The artist accentuates the encroaching rot through the
heavy use of black in the fruit itself, which is lightly
accentuated in yellow and capped by a dash of orange
at its tip. He further emphasizes the sexual connotations
of the banana's form by cradling it in the vase where,
devoid of shading to fix its placement in space, it appears
suspended. In contrast to the banana, the dish is pristine
and cool, its bisque-like surface created by the paper
itself. As in the earlier *Remains of Lunch* (pl. 26), other
compositional elements are subdivided into neatly
balanced sections. Two foliate divisions, brushed with
ink, abut the dish and are divided, like the graphite
design on the base, into three budding shapes, as are
the serrated edges of the leaf designs.

This softly veiled yet seemingly deliberate humaniza-
tion of still life forms was a quality shared by Kuniyoshi's
contemporaries. Demuth, for example, equated the eggplant in his *Eggplant and Peppers* (fig. 39) to "a heart—
maybe mine."[40] O'Keeffe's flower paintings and still lifes,
particularly following her 1923 exhibition at Anderson
Galleries, prompted critical speculation about how they
embodied the artist's femininity and sexuality.[41] Critics
also noted sexual associations of other modernists' still
lifes, as when Paul Rosenfeld described "a cold and
ferocious sensuality" in Hartley's still lifes, "with their
heavy stiff golden bananas, their dark luscious figs, their

erectile pears and enormous and breast-like peaches"
(fig. 40).[42]

A general preoccupation with psychoanalysis also
undoubtedly prompted Kuniyoshi to create works that
reflected, in Sherwood Anderson's words, "the new sex
consciousness." Kenneth Hayes Miller, the influential
teacher with whom Kuniyoshi studied at the Art Students
League between 1916 and 1920, was also caught up in
the fashion for Freud's theories, which had been introduced in the United States in 1909. Miller was known
to espouse Freudian readings regularly as part of his
teaching method.[43]

Despite this suggestive climate, the anthropomorphic qualities of Kuniyoshi's still lifes probably had less to
do with his own sexuality than with the larger realm of his
experiences as an immigrant. For example, the fruits in

FIG. 40
Marsden Hartley, *Movement No. 10*, 1917, oil on construction
board, 15¼ x 19⁹⁄₁₆ in. (38.8 x 49.7 cm), Art Institute of
Chicago, Alfred Stieglitz Collection

Grapes in White Bowl (1923, pl. 14) had personal connotations from his early days as a laborer in California:

> When I paint a bowl of grapes in my studio, I do it
> because grapes mean something to me. When I was
> a boy I spent many long hot summer days picking
> them. I used to go to the field very early, before
> sunrise, the air is cool then and vines and grapes are
> wet with dew. The big black bunches hang down so
> heavily, one on top of another. First thing I did was
> grab a soft slippery bunch and stuff as many into
> my mouth as it would hold. They were so juicy
> and cold.[44]

Kuniyoshi's still lifes of fruit probably reflect his American
environment, for while he was growing up in Japan, fruit
was of substandard quality, not plentiful, and likely un-
available for a family as poor as Kuniyoshi's. Bananas, for
example, would have seemed particularly exotic, because
tropical fruit was rare in Japan.[45]

Still lifes such as *Plant* (1925, pl. 32), *Leaves in a
Vase* (1924, pl. 18), *Pear* (1923, pl. 15), and *Orange*
(1925, pl. 20) emphasize the textures of organic forms
(plants and fruits) set against cool, rigid, man-made
ornamental objects (translucent ceramic). In *Pear* (pl. 15),
the undulating edges of the dish create a lively, rippling
effect. The interior of the dish is defined by ink wash
in gradations of tone that give it palpable animation.
Kuniyoshi left the paper blank at the edges of the fruit,
creating the halo effect he favored. The same dish plays
a central role in his contemporaneous painting, *Boy
Stealing Fruit* (pl. 5), where the boy—perhaps a surrogate
for the artist himself—lusts after the prized fruit, in this
case is a peach rather than a pear. In both works the fruit's
transforming anthropomorphic qualities underscore
Kuniyoshi's fascination with this subject. The peach in
Boy Stealing Fruit has the distinct aspect of voluptuous
buttocks. In *Pear*, the bulbous fruit which fills the dish at
some point approximated a human head in Kuniyoshi's
mind, for a preliminary sketch on the verso of the sheet
shows the fruit in the same dish transformed into a face
whose tongue mischievously sticks out at the viewer.

In these still lifes, Kuniyoshi employed a modernist
perspective that creates a slightly disjunctive relationship
between the primary subject and its container. Where the
artist earlier expressed this spatial ambiguity through a
disproportionate scale of plants and figures, in the still
lifes he uses the modernist conceit of a tilted plane and
the dissonance between two and three dimensions (see
fig. 34). In *Squash* (1924, pl. 19), Kuniyoshi contours
and models the vegetable's three-dimensional forms
against a decidedly two-dimensional plate whose wavy
border echoes the ridges of the squash. As a result, the
squash seems to levitate, as does the entire image on an
otherwise blank sheet of paper that extends well beyond
the compositional elements (the ratio of image to paper
is usually cropped in photographs). Kuniyoshi outlines
the squash with a controlled pen and ink line, while
bumpy nodules on the squash are modeled with a gray
ink wash. A touch of green highlights the stem.

Earlier in his career, Kuniyoshi had essayed a few
still life subjects such as the 1921 *Eggplant* (pl. 21), where
he employed a daring format of dark against dark and
accurately conveyed the rough, prickly stem and calyx
at the top of a freshly picked vegetable. The still lifes of
a few years later are more refined, set against light back-
grounds in a pristine environment "so neat and immacu-
late . . . that a wayward atom of otherwise innocuous dust
falling upon them would immediately be noticed as a
disturbing excrescence."[46] When Kuniyoshi added touches
of color, he did so selectively and, generally, naturalisti-
cally to provide the slightest points of definition. This
delicate coloration was reminiscent of Joseph Stella's
additions to his silverpoints around 1919 (see fig. 33),
and of traditional Japanese paintings that added faint
coloration to black and white images.

Kuniyoshi's high degree of control and refinement
earned his drawings almost universal praise during his
1923 annual exhibition at the Daniel gallery. Critics
commented upon his textures, design, and array of
tonalities, "from lu[s]cious blacks running the gamut
to the dead white of the background."[47] By his annual
Daniel exhibition the following year, Kuniyoshi's increas-
ingly sophisticated drawings were anointed his "pièce
de resistance" and "marvels of reserve and selection"
and compared to works by Odilon Redon: "they have
the same crisp vision and the sort of shading off of velvet

blacks into shiny whites that marks the work of the French visionary and which seems to hint that both artists read nature by flashes of lightning."[48]

The still lifes of 1925 point to Kuniyoshi's increasing attention to naturalism through observation—a quality that would characterize much of his work for the next several decades and for which his trip to France in the spring of 1925 seemed a turning point. In *Artichoke* (pl. 33), *Orange* (pl. 20), and *Plant* (pl. 32), he focuses on actual texture and expresses novelty through unusual contexts—a spiral of leaves surrounding the orange, the artichoke emerging from its stem, and a plant growing from a pot. The irregular circle of a dish showcases the orange; the lower portion of this shallow surface has a double edge and ink wash shading at the left edge to imply dimension, yet the fruit floats at the front of the picture plane. The orange's pitted surface is created through a buildup of ink.[49] Likewise, the burgeoning

artichoke in *Artichoke* is a precisely rendered illustration, outlined with a highly controlled and meticulous pen-and-ink line that imparts a crisp, sharp tip to the flower head's pointed, heart-shaped leaves. Adding further substance, graphite reinforces the edge of the stem and leaf, which are delicately brushed with ink wash, while the white paper serves as a contrasting highlight. *Artichoke* summarizes the sharp contrasts of crispness and depth that Kuniyoshi could achieve in his drawings, rendering restrained tones ranging from dense black to silver.

Although he continued to paint still lifes (fig. 41), Kuniyoshi largely abandoned the exhibition drawings. The artistic climate partially defeated the genre; Kuniyoshi later recalled: "Still life was never fashionable or artist felt it was important . . . I was very much aware in my student days that still lifes could be just as important."[50] In his later years, he lamented that drawing was not regarded as an independent entity: "Most often contemporary American

FIG. 41
Yasuo Kuniyoshi, *Weather Vane and Objects on a Sofa*, 1933, oil on canvas, 34 x 60 in. (86.4 x 152.4 cm),
Santa Barbara Museum of Art, gift of Wright S. Ludington

artists are not concerned with such drawings. . . . An artist usually regards his drawings as preparations for his paintings. . . . Drawing has generally been mistreated and ignored, so that as a legitimate work of art it receives neither support or encouragement."[51]

Kuniyoshi's drawings can now be given their proper due. Many forward-looking artists in the fascinating and complex decade of the 1920s were inspired by the ground-breaking American modernism of the previous decade. At the same time, they found great promise in indigenous subjects and their own unique voice. Kuniyoshi's ethnic background adds a fascinating component to the mix. Through his aesthetic choices, he affirmed his identity as both Japanese and American. In

embracing American subjects, he may have been heeding the words of Robert Coady, who in 1921 told a Penguin dinner: "It is time we got together and took things in our own hands, for the world today is in need of our culture. The European tragedy has practically made us the pivot of human progress."[52] Yet Kuniyoshi also sought to set himself apart in his drawings, both by choice of medium and by homage to his own native roots. He acknowledged the inherent yin and yang in the east/west dichotomy: "The ae[s]thetic impulse has these two aspects, but they relate to the same reality. They are opposite sides of the same coin."[53] Balancing the modern with the natural and mythical, Kuniyoshi expressed in his drawings a unique integration of rich aesthetic and cultural traditions.

Notes

· ·

1 Lloyd Goodrich, *Yasuo Kuniyoshi* (New York: Whitney Museum of American Art, 1948), p. 21. He never repeated a subject in another medium because, as he stated, "each subject should be created according to the medium one chooses to deal with." Anton Refregier, *Natural Figure Drawing* (New York: Tudor Publishing Company, 1948), p. 116.

2 Kuniyoshi also made drawings in preparation for lithographs. *Bather Under Water* (1924, lithographic crayon on transfer paper, Walker Art Center) was made for an unrealized lithograph; Yasuo Kuniyoshi to Norman Geske, May 28, 1949, File, Walker Art Center. Early in his career, Kuniyoshi also experimented with watercolors. He exhibited two at the Brooklyn Water Color Club's First Annual Exhibition, March 12-27, 1920.

3 When Lloyd Goodrich in 1948 asked Kuniyoshi which image came first, Goodrich noted that the artist "Thinks the oil 'Dream' was done before the drawing, but doesn't really remember—a guess. Says he never has done a painting from that kind of finished drawing." "Notes on Conversation with Kuniyoshi, January 13, 1948," Goodrich Archives in the Whitney Museum of American Art, Archives of American Art, Smithsonian Institution, reel N-670, frame 81 (hereafter Goodrich Archives, AAA).

4 For the drawings from 1944-53, see Tom Wolf, "The Late Drawings of Yasuo Kuniyoshi," *Drawing* 13 (January-February 1992): 100-103.

5 Jay Kaufman, *Globe and Commercial Advertiser*, January 17, 1922, p. 10.

6 Charles Daniel Papers, Archives of American Art, Smithsonian Institution, reel 1343, frame 39. Daniel's oral history is undated, but the correspondence with the interviewer, Dorothy Walker, is dated 1950-55. See Julie Mellby, *A Record of Charles Daniel and the Daniel Gallery* (M.A. thesis, City University of New York, Hunter College, 1993), p. 2, n. 2.

7 Field also collected Japanese prints and Old Master drawings, which he considered a "crucial part" of an artist's education. Doreen Bolger, "Hamilton Easter Field and His Contribution to American Modernism," *American Art Journal* 20, no. 2 (1988): 82-83.

8 Babette Deutsch, "The Soul of Wit," book reviews of Japanese poetry: *The "Uta"* by Arthur Waley and *Japanese Hokkus* by Yoné Noguchi, *Dial* 70 (February 1921): 207.

9 Among the most influential writings were those of Lafcadio Hearn, the offspring of an Anglo-Irish father and a Greek mother who spent the last fourteen years of his life in Japan. A prolific writer, he became one of the predominant interpreters of Japanese culture for the English reading audience, his popularity continuing well after his death in 1906.

10 Henry Tyrell, "Exhibitions That Forecast an Epidemic of Modernism," *New York World*, January 15, 1922, p. M7.

11 See Hamilton Easter Field, *Brooklyn Daily Eagle*, January 15, 1922; Henry Tyrell, *New York World*, March 12, 1922; Henry McBride, *New York Herald*, December 10, 1922, sect. 7, p. 7.

12 John Gould Fletcher, "The Secret of Far Eastern Painting," *Dial* 62 (January 11, 1917): 6.

13 "Notes on Conversation with Kuniyoshi, January 13, 1948," Goodrich Archives, AAA, reel N-670, frame 74. Among the Japanese artists he most revered were the famous ink painters Sesshu and Korin.

14 Much of the information on ink drawing techniques contained in this essay were provided by Judy Walsh, Senior Paper Conservator, National Gallery of Art, and Liz Lunning, Conservator of Works on Paper, The Menil Collection, Houston.

15 "Winslow Homer in his eyes is the greatest exponent of American art: he painted his own life, lived among the fishermen and was as they were. Thus can sincerity be maintained." W. H. de B. Nelson, "Sincerity in Art: Hamilton Easter Field," *International Studio* 59 (July 1916): xxv.

16 Carol Troyen, "A War Waged on Paper: Watercolor and Modern Art in America," in *Awash in Color: Homer, Sargent, and the Great American Watercolor* (Boston: Museum of Fine Arts, 1993), p. xlvii.

17 See Louis Bouché Papers, Archives of American Art, Smithsonian Institution (hereafter Bouché Papers, AAA), reel 688, frames 784-6.

18 Incised lines and gouged areas are common among Kuniyoshi's drawings. Fellow artist Karl Fortess recalls that Kuniyoshi used a razor to pick out selected elements of his designs. Author's conversation with Janis Conner and Joel Rosenkranz, November 17, 1994.

19 I am grateful to Marjorie B. Cohen, Fogg Art Museum, Harvard University, for her observations on Kuniyoshi's technique.

20 See, e.g., Nicholas Brigante's watercolor of Field's house, *New York from 110 Columbia Heights* (1923), in the Louis Newman Galleries brochure, "Nicholas Brigante, 1895-1989: A Survey" (Beverly Hills, 1992). I am grateful to Tom Wolf for bringing this drawing to my attention. Katherine Schmidt recalled that Field's Brooklyn Heights home looked down on the adjacent buildings and that it was built on the top of an incline. Interview with Katherine Schmidt, by Doreen Bolger, April 4, 1972, in curatorial files, Portland Museum of Art, Portland, Maine.

21 Sara Mazo Kuniyoshi, the artist's second wife, identified the utensil. She recalled that Kuniyoshi loved pear sauce and that the shaded area represents this favored condiment. Mary Lublin, conversation with the author, May 8, 1996.

22 Helen Appleton Read, "Alexander Brook at the Daniel Galleries," *Brooklyn Daily Eagle*, February 8, 1925, p. 2B. Alexander Brook interview, transcript, Oral History Program, Archives of American Art, Smithsonian Institution, p. 37. Betty Burroughs to Reginald Marsh, August 4, 1922, Reginald Marsh Papers, Archives of American Art (hereafter Marsh Papers, AAA), reel D-308, frame 45.

23 "An Interview with Peter Blume," *Visionary Company* 1 (Summer 1981): 64.

24 Bouché Papers, AAA, reel 688, frames 707, 708. Kuniyoshi echoed the same sentiments in Kuniyoshi, "East to West," *Magazine of Art* 33 (February 1940): 75.

25 Bouché Papers, AAA, reel 688, frame 860. Pascin's particularly risqué perspective was reflected in Henry McBride's headline in 1923, when Pascin's work was shown in a New York exhibition: "Naughty but Great," *New York Herald*, January 21, 1923, sect. 8, p. 7.

26 See, for instance, "Two Brooklynites in Diverse Exhibitions," *Brooklyn Daily Eagle*, January 13, 1924, sect. B, p. 2.

27 Betty Burroughs to Reginald Marsh, Marsh Papers, AAA, July 19, 1923, reel D-308, frame 93.

28 Goodrich Archives, AAA, reel N-668.

29 Kuniyoshi, "East to West," p. 75.

30 Yasuo Kuniyoshi to Reginald Marsh, June 14, 1922, Marsh Papers, AAA, D-308 frames 37-8.

31 I am deeply grateful to Barney Lipscomb, Robert J. O'Kennon, and the other staff members at the Botanical Research Institute of Texas, Fort Worth, for identifying the plants in Kuniyoshi's work.

32 The series is discussed in Nicolai Cikovsky Jr. and Franklin Kelly, *Winslow Homer* (Washington, D.C., and New Haven: National Gallery of Art and Yale University Press, 1995), pp. 116-117.

33 They graft together various plants, creating an odd appearance. Basil Hall Chamberlain, *Things Japanese, Being Notes on Various Subjects Connected with Japan* (London: John Murray, 1905), p. 175.

34 The quote is from an unidentified clipping in the Kuniyoshi Papers, Archives of American Art, Smithsonian Institution (hereafter Kuniyoshi Papers, AAA), reel D-176,

frame 97. See also Alexander Brook, "Yasuo Kuniyoshi," *Arts* 3 (February 1923): 126. In a review of Henrietta Shore and O'Keeffe, Helen Appleton Read ("In Studio and Gallery," *Shadowland* [May 1923]: 58) wrote: "Freud and Freudian complexes have been a byword with us for some time. Psycho-analysis has long since found its way into books and plays, but it has only recently been expressed in painting."

35 Bolger, "Field," p. 96. Elements of fantasy were also a primary motif in Marc Chagall's prints, drawings, and paintings of 1907-17. See Sandor Kuthy and Meret Meyer, *Marc Chagall 1907-1917* (Berne: Museum of Fine Arts, 1995).

36 "They were flying at San Domingo field near Los Angeles. Those machines were very old-fashioned. I went up a few times with an instructor, but everybody I knew got killed. So I stopped." "As They Are: 'Twenty-Eight Years,'" *Art News* 32, no. 26 (March 31, 1934): 13.

37 I am grateful to Judy Walsh for pointing out this technical parallel.

38 Basil Hall Chamberlain noted the Japanese "take little account [of wildflowers] which is strange; for the hills and valleys of their beautiful country bear them in profusion." *Things Japanese*, p. 174. One Japanese legend, "The Love of Asagao," describes how the morning glory was esteemed for its beauty; see F. Hadland Davis, *Myths and Legends of Japan* (1913; reprint, New York: Dover Publications, Inc., 1992), p. 249.

39 Kuniyoshi told Lloyd Goodrich that the color in the early drawings was colored ink. Goodrich Archives, AAA, reel N-670, frame 82. The earliest known drawing to contain this subdued coloration is *Flowers in Vase* (1922, unlocated). See Goodrich Archives, reel N-668, frame 536.

40 Quoted in Troyen, "A War Waged on Paper," p. xlii.

41 For a thorough discussion of the response to O'Keeffe's work in the 1920s, see Barbara Buhler Lynes, *O'Keeffe, Stieglitz and the Critics, 1916-1929* (Ann Arbor: UMI Research Press, 1989).

42 Paul Rosenfeld, "American Painting," *Dial* 71 (December 1921): 658.

43 Sherwood Anderson to Paul Rosenfeld, August 10, 1924, in *Paul Rosenfeld, Voyager in the Arts*, ed. by Jerome Mellquist and Lucie Wiese (New York: Creative Age Press, 1948), p. 224. On Miller's teaching, see Alexander Brook, interview by Paul Cummings, July 7-8, 1977, transcript, Oral History Program, Archives of American Art.

44 Yasuo Kuniyoshi, "Universality in Art," *League Quarterly* 20, no. 3 (Spring 1949): 7. (The undated typescript of this article is in Goodrich Archives, AAA, reel N-670, frames 6-7.)

45 Chamberlain, *Things Japanese*, pp. 179-180. According to Ritsuko T. Ozawa, Curator, Yasuo Kuniyoshi Museum, Okayama, the Kuniyoshi family was exceedingly poor. Letter to author, May 2, 1996.

46 Alexander Brook, "Yasuo Kuniyoshi," *Arts* 5 (January 1924): 27.

47 *New York Evening Post*, January 27, 1923.

48 *New York Evening Post*, January 12, 1924, p. 15; *Brooklyn Daily Eagle*, January 13, 1924, sect. B, p. 2; and Henry McBride, "Modern Art," *Dial* 76 (March 1924): 295-296.

49 Another unlocated drawing of an orange on its branch is reproduced in the Goodrich Archives, AAA, reel N-668, frame 600.

50 Kuniyoshi Papers, AAA, undated, unmicrofilmed, pp. 10C-10D.

51 Refregier, *Natural Figure Drawing*, p. 116.

52 *Arts* 1, no. 2 (January 1921): 34.

53 Kuniyoshi, "Universality in Art," p. 7.

Index

· ·

Reproductions of works are indicated by italic page numbers

A
· ·

Adam and Eve (The Fall of Man), *1*, 28-29, *29*, 55, 61

After the Bath, *7*, 30-31, 32

Ama Dressing Her Hair on the Sea Shore (U. Kuniyoshi), 36-37, *37*

Armory Show of 1913, 21, 23

art colonies, summer, 24, 58

Arts, The (magazine), 34

Art Students League, 21-22, 24, 25-26, 56, 63

Artichoke, *54*, 65

Ault, George, 32

B
· ·

Baby and Toy Cow, 27, *44*, 58, 59

Baby Frightened by Water, 32

Bacon, Peggy, 56

Bad Dream, 35, *51*, 60-61

Bather with Cigarette, *10*, 32

Bedroom, *48*, 58-59

Bellows, George, 22

Belmaison Gallery of Decorative Arts, 58

Benton, Thomas Hart, 26

Black Curtain, The. See *Bedroom*

Blanch, Arnold, 25-26

Blaue Reiter, Der, 26, 33

Bloch, Albert, 26, 41 n.20

Boss, Homer, 21

Bouché, Louis, 23, 30, 41 n.7, 58, 59

Boy Feeding Chickens, 31, *32*

Boy Frightened by Lightning, 26-27, *27*

Boy Frightened by Snake, 26, *27*

Boy Stealing Fruit, vii, *5*, 31, 64

Boy with Cow, *46*, 60

Bradley, John, 31

Brancusi, Constantin, 23

Braque, George, 32

Brodzky, Horace, 23

Brook, Alexander, 22, 23, 26, 30, 31, 59

Brooklyn Heights art community, 23, 24, 58, 59, 67 n.20

Burchfield, Charles, 56

Burroughs, Betty, 59

Burty, Philippe, 34

C
· ·

Calder, Alexander, 23, 24

Calf Doesn't Want to Go, The, 29, *46*, 60

Campendonk, Heinrich, 26, 36

Captain's Daughter. See *After the Bath*

Cézanne, Paul, 22, 55

Chagall, Marc, 36

Child, *30*, 31

Christian iconography, 22, 28-29, 32

Coady, Robert, 66

Cock and Snake, 28

Cove, The (Spencer), 28, *28*

Cows in Pasture, *6*, 59, 60

Crabs [Crab and Rocks at Ebb Tide] (U. Kuniyoshi), 36, *36*

Crucifixion [Modern Crucifix], 22, *23*

Cubism, 28, 36, 59

D
· ·

Dadaism, 59

Daniel, Charles, 26, 56

Daniel Gallery, 26, 28, 29, 30, 32, 37, 41 n.18, 55, 56, 59, 62

Daumier, Honoré, 22, 41 n.6, 42 n.49

Davis, Stuart, 21

Demuth, Charles, 26, 31, 56, 59, 62, 63

Deskey, Donald, 38

Dickinson, Preston, 59

Dish with Banana, *16*, 30, 63

Dove, Arthur, 23, 55

Dow, Arthur Wesley, 56

drawing,
    as preparation for painting, 55-56, 66
    popularity as medium, 55-56, 65-66

Dream (painting), *2*, 29, 36, 55, 61, 67 n.3

Dream, The (drawing), 29, 35, *50*, 55, 60, 61, 67 n.3

Duchamp, Marcel, 23, 32, 59

Duffy, Edmund, 25

E
· ·

Eggplant, 27, 30, *43*, 64

Eggplant and Peppers (Demuth), 63, *63*

Eilshemius, Louis, 32

Einstein Child, The. See *Child*

Expressionism, 26, 36

F

Faggi, Alfeo, 40

Fantin-Latour, Henri, 24

Fenellosa, Ernest, 56

Field, Hamilton Easter,
    as art critic, 28, 34, 35-36, 61
    as collector, 27, 58, 59, 61, 67 n.7
    friendship and support for Kuniyoshi, 23-24, 25, 26,
        28, 33, 34, 35-36, 56, 59
    interest in Japanese art, 34, 40
    support for contemporary artists, 23-25, 28, 30, 31, 40, 58

Fireman's Dinner for Brancusi (Calder), 23, *24*

Fish and Seaweed, 8, 36

Fisherman, 36, *52,* 62

Flower Study #1 (Demuth), 62, *62*

folk art, American, 21, 26, 27, 28, 31, *32,* 33, 34, 59

Forbidden Fruit, vi, vii

Force, Juliana, 31, 40

Freudian psychology, 61, 63, 68 n.34

Futurism, 23

G

Gaudier-Brzeska, Henri, 23

Gaylor, Wood, 23

Gérôme, Jean-Léon, 24

Girl on Sofa, 55, *55*

Glackens, William, 26

Goodrich, Lloyd, 22, 41 n.7

Grapes in White Bowl, 14, 30, 64

Greco-Roman traditions, 29, 40

Green Apple on Black Plate (O'Keeffe), 57, *57*

Growing Weeds, 61-62, *61*

Gyokuen, Bompo, 38, 39

H

Hartley, Marsden, 24, 26, 27, 33, 41 n.21, 63

Haviland family, 34

Henri, Robert, 21, 26

Hill, W. E., 31

Hirsch, Stefan, 25

Homer, Winslow, 58, 60, 67 n.15

Hopper, Edward, 22, 32-33, 56

Howland, Isabella, 25

I

Impressionists, 24, 25, 33

Inukai, Kyohei, 34, 35

Island House, The (Woodbury), 24-25, *25*

J

Japan, American fascination with, 56, 67 n.9

Japanese artistic tradition, 22, 26, 27, 28, 29, 33, 34, 35,
    36-37, 38, 56-57, 62, 64

K

Karfiol, Bernard, 25, 30, 32, 36

Korin, Ogata, 35, 42 n.49, 67 n.13

Kroll, Leon, 30

Kuhn, Walt, 23, 30, 32, 36, 59

Kuniyoshi, Utagawa, 36-37, 38

Kuniyoshi, Yasuo, *frontis.*
    artistic training, 21-22, 27, 33, 41 n. 6
    critics' reaction to work, 26, 28, 29-30, 33, 34, 55, 56, 57
    depictions of animals, 29, 36-37, 38, 42 n.52, 62
    depictions of children, 26-27, 29, 31, 58, 60
    depictions of cows, 26, 29, 58, 59-61
    depictions of plants, 36, 38, 40, 60, 61-62
    depictions of women, 30, 32-33, 37, 55, 61
    drawing technique, 21, 26, 27, 29-30, 36, 55, 57, 58,
        62-63, 64-65, 67 nn.3,18
    early years in Japan, vi, 21, 27, 29, 57, 64
    early years in United States, vi, 21-22, 33, 61, 63-64
    exhibitions with Daniel Gallery, 26, 28, 29, 34, 37,
        41 n.18, 56, 57, 60, 64-65
    exhibitions with Society of Independent Artists, 22, 23
    fantasy in subject matter, vii, 29, 35-36, 55, 60-61
    fusion of Japanese and American influences in art, vi-vii,
        27-28, 33, 34, 36-40, 55, 57, 58, 62, 66
    humor in paintings and drawings, 29, 59-60
    influence of Japanese heritage, 21, 22, 26, 27, 28, 29-30,
        33, 35, 36, 38, 60, 61, 62, 64
    landscapes by, 25, 26, 27, 42 n.53
    later work, vi, vii, 42 n.52, 55, 59, 60, 65-66
    marriage to Katherine Schmidt, 25-26, 59
    painting technique, 21, 24, 26, 29, 30-31, 32-33, 35, 36
    photographic work, 26, 35
    religious iconography in works, 22, 26, 28-29, 32, 35
    sexual allusions in artworks, 30, 37, 63, 64
    still life subjects, 27, 30, 33, 63-64, 65
    summers in Ogunquit, 24, 25, 26, 60, 61-62
    travel to France, vii, 40, 55

L

Lachaise, Gaston, 30

Lady Slipper, 17, 38, 63

Landscape, 26, *26,* 29

Landscape in Haboku Style (Sesshu), 38, *39*

Landscape with Figures (Miller), 22, *22*

Laurent, Robert, 24, 25, 30, 40

Leaves, 61, *61*

Leaves in a Vase, 18

Life Saver, 9, 33

Lighthouse Hill (Hopper), 32, *33*

Little Girl in Lavender, 31, *31*

M

Maine Family, 4, 25, 59

Man Ray, 26, 59

Marin, John, 55

Marsh, Reginald, 32, 59

Matisse, 55

Mauro, John, 32

McBride, Henry, 29, 33, 42 n.47

Miller, Kenneth Hayes, 22, 25, 26, 33, 34, 41 n.6, 42 n.42, 63

Modern Crucifix. See *Crucifixion*

modernism, American, 21, 22, 23, 24, 26, 27, 30, 38, 55, 61, 64

modernism, European, 26, 32, 33, 40, 57

Moon and Melon (Chu Ta), 57, *57*

Morning Glory and Weeds, 49, 61, 62

Murrell, William, 28

N

Nadelman, Elie, 30

National Academy of Design, 22, 23

New York, as art center, 21-24. *See also* Brooklyn Heights arts community, Belmaison Gallery, Daniel Gallery, Penguin, Society of Independent Artists

nudes, in modernist art, 30

O

Octopus, 38, *38*

Octopus Clutching a Rock (U. Kuniyoshi), 38, *38*

Ogunquit, Maine, *frontis. 24, 25,* 24-25, 59, 62
    art colony, 24-25, 27, 28, 30, 58

Okayama, Japan, vi, vii, 21, 29, 62

O'Keeffe, Georgia, 23, 40, 55, 56, 57, 58, 63

Old Masters, influence in 20th-century art, 22, 33, 34

Orange, 20, 57, 64, 65

Orchids and Rock (Gyokuen), 38, *39*

P

Pascin, Jules, 23, 30, 59, 68 n.25

Pear, 15, 64

Penguin club, 23, 30, 32, 41 n.7, 59, 66

Peonies (Stella), 56, *56*

Picasso, Pablo, 23, 24, 30, 32, 40

Pierce, Waldo, 32

Plant, 53, 64, 65

Post-Impressionism, 33, 57

Precisionism, 28

R

Radio City Music Hall murals, 38, *39,* 40

realism, European, 32, 35

Redon, Odilon, 29, 61, 64-65

Reflection (Inukai), 34, *35*

Remains of Lunch, 47, 59, 63, 68 n.21

Renaissance influence in art, 22, 26, 27, 33, 34, 37, 40

Renoir, 22

Revelation, vii, *vii*

Rousseau, Henri, 36, 40

Ryder, Albert Pinkham, 22, 25

S

Salons of America exhibitions, 31

Sargent, John Singer, 25, 35

Schmidt, Katherine, *frontis.,* 22, 23, 24, 25-26, 31, 40, 58, 61-62, 67 n.20

Schnakenberg, Henry, 31

Self-Portrait as a Photographer, 12, 26, 34-35

Sesshu, 38, 39, 42 n.49, 67 n.13

Sheeler, Charles, 26, 31, 32, 34, 56, 59

Shinrai (Thunder God), 35, 42 n.49

Shinrai, 35

Sleeping Beauty, 37, *37*

Sloan, John, 31

Society of Independent Artists, 22-23, 31

Spencer, Niles, 25, 28, 29, 32, 34, 36, 59

Squash, 19, 33-34, 64

Stella, Joseph, 23, 32, 56, 64

Sterne, Maurice, 24

Stieglitz, Alfred, 55, 56

sumi ink drawing, 27, 38, 57

Surrealism, 29

Swamp Lily (Laurent), *40*

Swimmer, The, 11, 32

T

Tatsume Kaze (Wind God), 35, 42 n.49

Three Cows and One Calf, 29, *45,* 60

Thurnscoe, Maine, 25, *25,* 28

Thurnscoe School of Modern Art, 24

U

Upstream, 3, 59

V

Varian, Dorothy, 25

Vase of Flowers (Hartley), 27, *28*

Virginie Combing Her Hair (Karfiol), 30, *30*

Vorticism, 23

W

Waitresses from the Sparhawk, 13, 32-33

Walkowitz, Abraham, 55

Weber, Max, 23, 24

Weeds and Sun, 36, *36*

Whitney Studio Club, 31

Woodbury, Charles, 24-25

Woodstock, New York, 24

Z

Zayas, Mario de, 32